KEVIN'S BED

BERNARD FARRELL

MERCIER PRESS

MERCIER PRESS
PO Box 5, 5 French Church Street, Cork
16 Hume Street, Dublin 2

Trade enquiries to CMD DISTRIBUTION,
55a Spruce Avenue, Stillorgan Industrial Park, Blackrock, Dublin

ISBN 1 85635 286 2

10 9 8 7 6 5 4 3 2 1

This book is published with the financial assistance of The Arts Council, An
Chomhairle Ealaíon, Ireland.

The Arts Council
An Chomhairle Ealaíon

Printed in Ireland by Colour Books Ltd.

PREFACE

For any playwright, it is always a cause for celebration (if not hysteria!) when, on finishing one play, he or she looks into the barrel and discovers that it is not empty, that there is still something else down there that demands to be written.

In June 1996, two things happened to me that had me looking into that barrel – and praying that I would not see the bottom. I had finished one play (*Stella By Starlight* for the Gate Theatre) and, within weeks, I was appointed Writer-in-Association with the Abbey Theatre. This honour had a two-fold aspect: one was financial (thanks to Anglo Irish Bank) and the other was a commission to write a new play for the Abbey stage ... assuming that I had a new play within me!

Thankfully – and with much relief – the barrel revealed not only a subject, but an almost ready-made plot. In fact – as only occasionally happens – it was an idea so well developed that it seemed to have always been there, awaiting its moment.

I knew, for example, that the play would be about a family and would trace the parents' expectations, disappointments and broken dreams and, in doing so, would mainly concern itself with the fortunes of their younger son, the doomed dreamer called Kevin.

The title was also there from the beginning – Kevin would make his bed and have to lie in it. The problem was how to spread the action over so many years of his life. This stopped me in my tracks. Eventually, I realised that if the first act could be on his parent's Silver Anniversary and the second act on their Golden, that would set the ground to chart the changes over a twenty-five year span.

With that resolved, it was now time to meet Patrick Mason, the Artistic Director of the Abbey, to confirm that I did indeed have a play and could now outline the plot.

I have never been good at describing work-in-progress, or, in this case, work-still-in-my head – and I remember sitting in Patrick's office and giving him what must have been the most confused, garbled, unimpressive synopsis he had probably ever heard. But he listened carefully, questioned me occasionally, and then not only encouraged me to go off and write it but, months later, continued to send me little postcards of support and enquiry.

The play was written in the late spring, summer and early autumn of 1997. Throughout this time, sub-plots continually presented themselves for consideration. Kevin's brother John had his story, as had Kevin's childhood sweetheart Betty, as had his Italian wife Maria and even the inner lives of the neighbours (seen and unseen) began to emerge. But always, at the heart of the play, were Dan and Doris, Kevin's parents, forever puzzled and perplexed, amused and appalled at how their happiness was at the mercy of their children's fortunes. Gradually, the play had become the story of their survival.

When I finished a final draft and Patrick had expressed his enthusiasm, the next move was to choose a director. Ben Barnes and I had worked together on six of my previous plays and, by now, we could almost read each other's thoughts. I knew that he would not only immediately understand the main thrust of the play, but would enthusiastically search out and explore the darker layers that lurked, often unspoken, beneath the comedy. And so, I was delighted when he agreed to direct.

Kevin's Bed opened at the Abbey in April 1998 with a cast to die for. On the night, all seemed to fall into place and the reception and critical response were both wonderful ... and the optimists predicted that *Kevin* could have a long life.

I just hoped that he would survive the run. But, months later, his future looked even brighter when the Abbey took the play on a very successful national tour and, in 1999, staged its revival back at the Abbey. In between, I had the pleasure of seeing its Scottish premier at the Citizens Theatre in Glasgow and its US premier is planned for March 2000.

All of which seems far removed from the day when I looked into the barrel and, with more hope than confidence, wondered if I would find anything at all. And, having found Kevin, agonised if I would ever manage to simultaneously look back and forward through the timeframes of twenty-five years – back to childhood where all seems possible and then into the future where the best-laid plans may come to nought. And, throughout, explore the play's characters as they deal with each unrealised dream.

And now, with *Kevin* out in the world, it is nice to look back at his beginnings – and, with this publication, forward to where and when he may be again revived, re-explored and, hopefully, enjoyed by new audiences.

BERNARD FARRELL

DEDICATION
FOR GLORIA

Kevin's Bed was first produced at the Abbey Theatre Dublin on 29 April 1998 with the following cast:

Kevin	David Parnell
Doris	Barbara Brennan
Dan	Eamon Morrissey
Cecily	Lisa Harding
John	Seán Rocks
Pauline	Marion O'Dwyer
Betty	Catherine Walsh
Maria	Carmen Hanlon
Young Kevin	Cormac Doddy or Mark Ryan
Young Betty	Jessica Barnes or Katie Monnelly

Director	Ben Barnes
Designer	Frank Hallinan Flood
Lighting	Tony Wakefield

For its subsequent national tour, the cast changes were:

Dan	Des Keogh
Maria	Ilaria D'Elia
Cecily	Renee Weldon

Characters

Doris, aged 46 and 71
Dan, aged 47 and 72
Kevin, their son, aged 22 and 47
John, their son, aged 24 and 49
Pauline, a friend, aged 40 and 65
Betty, aged 19 and 44
Maria, aged 20 and 45
Cecily, aged 24
Young Kevin, aged 12
Young Betty, aged 9

KEVIN'S BED

A large, old-fashioned kitchen. In back wall, from S/L, the back door, next a large window without curtains, then a dumb-waiter with its door closed. Beneath the window, a sink, cupboards etc. Beyond the window, strangely, there is just darkness.

In S/R wall, from up-stage, a door to a fuel-room that houses coal and logs. Next, a fuel-burning range. Next, a door to the hallway, off.

Throughout the room, religious pictures, one of Pope Paul VI and a Child-of-Prague statue. Over the door to the hallway, a set of room-bells.

The house is large, old and well-kept. We see it now as it was twenty-five years ago. It is 3.00p.m.

(In the opening sequence of the play, the light is strange: Darkness outside, and inside, the light is streaked across the walls. In short, a hint of abnormality. Also, in this sequence, the dialogue may not reflect what we see. This will all be explained later.)

Now, we hear the opening of Jo Stafford and Gordon Mc-Crae singing Whispering Hope. *Establish and fade as Kevin appears outside the back window, coming towards the back door. He is 47, an unsure man, eager to please. He wears glasses. Behind him come his elderly parents: Doris (aged 71) and Dan (aged 72) who is on a walking stick. Both are well-dressed for the occasion: their Fiftieth Wedding Anniversary.*

In speech and demeanour, Doris seems more refined than Dan – reflecting different backgrounds.

Dan: *(Outside)* Maybe we should have knocked at the front door?

11

Kevin: *(Outside)* It's all right, Da, come on in. *(Now enters. Calls).* Hel-lo? Hello ladies?

Doris: *(Coming in with Dan. Suddenly)* Oh my God!

Kevin: *(Anxiously)* What is it, Ma?

Doris: Will you look what they've done to the kitchen.

Kevin: *(Looking)* What?

Doris: They've destroyed it. Dan, look what they've done – they've destroyed the kitchen.

Dan: *(Painfully)* Doris, all this travelling has me hips nearly dislocated.

Doris: *(Of the stage-right wall)* And what kind of pictures are these?

Kevin: Now, Ma, don't start – times change and places change too – don't be remembering it as it was, see it as it is.

Dan: Kevin, is it all right if I sit down somewhere?

Kevin: Yes, Da, anywhere you like. *(Calls)* Hello?

Doris: And where are my lovely bells?

Kevin: Ma, you're here for your anniversary, not to go poking around. *(Opens the kitchen door).* Hello?

Doris: *(At the fuel-room door)* What has she got in here?

Dan: *(Indicates outside)* That wall is blocking out your light, son.

Kevin: That wall has nothing to do with me, Da.

Doris: *(At the fuel-room)* A washing machine! What's a washing machine doing in here?

Kevin: It's now a laundry room, Ma – and I wish you'd stop ...

Doris: And where's the fuel for the range?

Kevin: Just sit down!

Doris: *(Of the range)* Don't tell me this is now a dud!

Dan: *(Of outside)* There's no need for that wall to be

so high.

Kevin: *(Patiently)* Da, that wall has nothing to do with me.

Doris: *(The range)* It *is* a dud. Dan, the range is now a dud.

Kevin: It's not – it's converted to electricity – and will you please leave everything alone ...

Doris: The whole place is destroyed.

Dan: That wall is preventing you from seeing the apple trees.

Kevin: Da, they cut down the apple trees to build the bungalows.

Dan: What? You let them cut down the ...?

Kevin: *(Furious)* I didn't let anyone do anything be- cause I don't live here and neither do you.

Dan: Doris, they cut down the apple trees to build the bungalows ...

Doris: They've destroyed everything.

Kevin: *(Angrily decides)* Right! That's it! Come on, all out and we'll go back around and knock on the front door, before someone walks in and catch- es us ...

Doris: But why is there no one here to meet us?

Kevin: *(Ushering)* I don't know, Ma. Come on, Da – we're going round the front.

Dan: We should've done that in the first place.

Doris: *(Going)* You were always too soft, Kevin, letting everybody walk on you ...

Kevin: All right, Ma – and, remember, when we come around the front, pretend you've never been in here or seen anything ...

Dan: *(Going)* I'm supposed to take it easy – these

	plastic knees don't last forever.

Kevin: Do you hear me, Da? – don't pretend you've seen anything when they bring us in here ...

Dan: Yes, yes, yes, I've seen nothing.

Kevin: Have you got that too, Ma? – look surprised when you see it.

Doris: Surprised? – I'll be physically sick if I have to look at it again.

(As Kevin ushers them out, the kitchen door opens and Cecily comes in. She is 24, now in a dressing-gown and a towel around her head – just out of the shower. She carries an empty linen basket. She now suddenly sees them, panics, drops the linen basket and screams)

Cecily: *(Panic)* Oh my God!

Kevin: *(Quickly)* It's all right, Cecily, it's only us.

Cecily: *(Calls in panic)* Mum ... !

Kevin: *(Sternly)* Cecily! Stop it! It's me – Da!

Cecily: *(Stops)* Dad? *(Angrily searching for her glasses in her dressing-gown)* What are you doing here ... ? *(Has found her glasses. Now sees)* Oh my God it's not Grandma and Granddad already, is it?

Kevin: Of course, it's Grandma and Granddad.

Dan: It is, Cecily *(Remembers)* but we haven't been in here yet ...

Kevin: *(Sharply)* Da, Cecily has now seen us. Ma, you recognise Cecily ...

Doris: Well of course I do – hello, Cecily, love.
(Kisses Cecily)

Cecily: Hello Grandma, hello Granddad. *(Anxiously to Kevin)* Dad, why are they here?

Kevin: For God's sake – it's their anniversary.

Cecily:	But *now!* Mum says we won't start until five and it's not even three yet.
Kevin:	Five? I was told half-three because they have to be back in that place before nine.
Cecily:	But Mum left a message on your machine this morning, saying it was changed to five.
Kevin:	This morning I was on my way to Athlone to collect them.
Doris:	Kevin, the caretaker would have arranged transport if it was too much ... (for you to come and collect us)
Kevin:	It's all right, Ma, you're here now and no problem. *(To Cecily)* Right – where's your mother?
Cecily:	She's upstairs in the bathroom, having a soak.
Doris:	A drink?
Cecily:	No, a soak in the bath.
Kevin:	Right. I'll go up to her, get it sorted out. And Ma, Da, you wait here and relax *(Upbeat)* ... after all, this is your big day, a chance to meet all your old friends, few songs, few laughs, just like old times. Back in a minute. *(Goes)*
Doris:	*(Awkwardly)* Fifty years today. Our Golden.
Cecily:	Yes. And I've invited lots of my friends over to make up the numbers.
Doris:	Yes – not many of our old gang left.
Dan:	Cecily, is it all right if I sit down here again?
Cecily:	Oh yes, please do.
Dan:	*(Realises)* I don't mean 'again' of course, because I haven't been sitting here before or even *in* here before, before now that is – in fact, it's nearly twelve years since ...
Doris:	Just sit down, Dan.

Dan: Right. *(Quietly, as he sits)* You move, you're in agony; stay still and you'll get a blood clot.

Cecily: *(Then)* So what do you think? Does it bring back memories – your old house?

Doris: Oh it's much nicer now – isn't it, Dan?

Dan: *(Too much)* What? Oh yes. Great improvement all round.

Cecily: Yes, lots of changes – and more when this baby arrives.

Doris: *(More downbeat)* Oh yes.

Cecily: But I'm not showing, am I?

Doris: *(Not enthusiastic)* No, you're not.

Cecily: It'll be the next big party here – after your's to-day.

Doris: I suppose.

Dan: *(Hard)* And is there any chance of the father turning up for that, do you think?
(The kitchen door opens – Kevin returns)

Kevin: *(Upbeat)* Okay, everything's terrific. Now, I think, maybe, Cecily, you might bring Grandma and Granddad ...

Cecily: And you saw mum, did you?

Kevin: *(Stops)* What? No, she was having her soak and the bathroom door was locked ... but I'll see her later. *(Upbeat again)* But now, as we have a few hours, time for you to relax before it all begins – so maybe, Cecily, you'd take Grandma and Granddad somewhere comfortable ...

Cecily: Yes, why don't we go to the morning-room.

Doris: *(Quietly to Dan)* The morning-room!

Kevin: Great. Perfect.

Cecily: *(Going, to Doris)* All this must bring back mem-

16

	ories of your Silver Anniversary – that was here too, wasn't it?
Doris:	Oh yes – twenty-five years ago.
Cecily:	And do you remember it well? *(Goes)*
Doris:	Oh, only too well. *(Hard to Kevin)* Thanks to some people.
Kevin:	*(Hushed)* For God's sake – don't start dragging that up.
Doris:	*(Hard)* And why not? Wasn't that the day you made your bed – and haven't you had us all sleeping in it ever since.
Cecily:	*(Looking back in)* Grandma, I thought you were behind me.
Doris:	*(Politely)* No, still admiring the kitchen.
Cecily:	You're still to see the rest of the house. *(Goes again)*
Doris:	*(Flatly)* I can't wait. *(Goes)*
Dan:	*(Going)* Don't mind her too much, son – she's only afraid we'll have a repetition of all the hullabaloo at the Silver Anniversary.
Kevin:	We won't, Da.
Dan:	I hope not, Kevin – *(A warning)* – because I wouldn't like her put through that again.
Kevin:	I know, Da – and she won't be.
Dan:	*(Hard)* Good.
	(Dan goes, closing the kitchen door. Kevin looks around. He goes to the back door. Above it, he notices a set of hanging chimes. They once tinkled in the breeze – now old and broken. He stands on a chair to get them. He holds them, tinkles them, remembering. He then throws them into a drawer – yet beyond the kitchen door, he can still hear them tinkling. So can we.

Now, as he remembers, the room brightens. The light is now natural within the room. Outside the window, it is a summer's afternoon, sunny and bright, revealing the large garden of apple and pear trees. Here, also, a garden swing.

Kevin pulls his tie loose and removes his glasses. He looks more youthful. He is now aged 22 – but as unsure/nervous as ever. The kitchen door opens and John, his older brother, aged 24, comes in. He is carrying the chimes, as new. He is a lively, assured, young man.

It is twenty-five years ago and we are back to the house, exactly as we see it now, for the Silver Anniversary. Beyond, whenever the kitchen door is opened, we can hear the sounds of a party in full swing. Now, they are lustily singing I'd Like to Teach the World to Sing)

John: *(Merrily)* Kevin! What are you doing in here – praying?

Kevin: *(Nervously)* What? No, no, just ... What's that?

John: Betty brought it for the folks – silver for the Silver Anniversary. Ma said I'm to hang it up somewhere. Over the door, eh?

Kevin: Yes. Good idea.

John: How do you think she's looking?

Kevin: Ma?

John: No – Betty.

Kevin: Oh great, terrific.

John: *(Hanging the chimes)* And you know she's now permanent in the bank?

Kevin: Really?

John: Oh yes – she heard exactly one week after I got

	my post of responsibility at the school. Did we celebrate that night? – leave it to your imagination. *(Of the chimes over the door)* How's that?
Kevin:	Great. And when will you and Betty be getting, you know ... mar ... mar ... ?
John:	'Married', Kevin – it's not a sin to say it. But no rush – anyway I can't just walk out of here, leave Ma and Da and Granny and all that.
Kevin:	No.
John:	Though, now that you're home, might make my escape. Now, what else was I to do? Yes, a few logs into the range. *(Closes the kitchen door)* It's going a bomb in there – great crowd, a great day for Ma and Da. You should go in, Kevin – they all want to see you.
Kevin:	*(Nervously)* Yes, I will.
John:	*(Getting logs from the fuel-room for the range)* Look, if it's any consolation – I do know how you feel.
Kevin:	*(Gloomily)* Do you?
John:	Well actually I don't – but only because I'd never have gone off to be a priest, too fond of a-bit-of-the-other for that – but, fair dues, you gave it a try, you lived in Rome, you can speak Latin, you got a degree for free – there's a lot of positives to all this, Kevin.
Kevin:	Oh sure.
John:	No, there is! Okay, Ma and Da are disappointed ...
Kevin:	They've hardly looked at me all day.
John:	*(Harder)* Well, can you blame them – the way you went about telling them you'd left?
Kevin:	I didn't know how to tell them.

John: (*Harder*) So you disappear in Europe for four weeks and suddenly turn up here yesterday and drop the bombshell!

Kevin: I had to turn up for their anniversary ...

John: (*Hard*) But they have telephones in Italy, haven't they? – you could have warned them you were out.

Kevin: (*Louder*) All right! I know! I said I'm sorry!

John: (*Suddenly calm*) Okay, right, sure. So now that's all in the past, over and done, you've made your decision – made your bed, as Ma says – you're out, you're here, and we'll have to get used to it.

Kevin: (*Nervously*) Except, John ...

John: No, Kevin, except nothing!, that's it! – this is Ma and Da's big day, so no more upsets ... (*Upbeat*) and, listen, you should be in there ... there's talent in there, well-stacked talent ... and women fancy you – they do! – so let's show them all you're back in circulation and raring to go ...

Kevin: No, I can't.

John: (*Grabs Kevin, merrily*) Course you can – get them off you, girls!

Kevin: (*Resisting*) No, not now!

John: (*Singing*) 'It's now or never ...'

Kevin: (*Angrily pulls free*) No, I said I can't – I have to stay here because ...

John: (*Angrily*) Because what? Because you want to feel sorry for yourself?

Kevin: No – because there's someone coming to see me, to talk to me and I need time to think of what I'm going to say.

John:	*(Stops)* Say to who?
Kevin:	To this person who's coming. She phoned this morning. That was the call I took when ...
John:	She?!
Kevin:	Originally she was coming tomorrow but now she's coming today because of flights or something and I don't know how to tell anyone and that's why I'm out here trying to work it all out in my head before ...
John:	There's a woman coming to see you? Do I know this woman?
Kevin:	No, she's an Italian.
John:	An Italian? And where's she coming from?
Kevin:	*(Annoyed)* Where do Italians usually come from? Italy! Rome.
John:	*(Suspicious)* And what does she want?
Kevin:	I told you – she wants to see me, to talk to me ...
John:	*(Suddenly. Angrily)* Wait a minute – Jesus Christ, don't tell me this is a mot.
Kevin:	*(Nervously)* No, no ...
John:	Don't tell me this is some young wan you had in Italy when we all thought you were studying for the priesthood?
Kevin:	No, no, for God's sake, she's a nun.
John:	*(Stops)* A nun?
Kevin:	A nun. A clerical counsellor. Sent over. Ever since ... since the Second Vatican Council they give nuns all kinds of tasks to involve them more in the working of the Church and especially in the Church's mission to recruit and to ... counsel and console.
John:	*(Realising)* Oh right. And what's wrong with

21

	telling us all this?
Kevin:	It's Ma and Da – they're so disappointed already that I didn't want ...
John:	But Ma would be delighted to hear about a nun coming from Rome to see you – you know she loves nuns and priests and bishops ...
Kevin:	But Da – I didn't want him roaring about me changing my mind again ...
John:	He won't. What's her name, this nun?
Kevin:	Sister Maria.
John:	But that's great, there's no problem there. Christ, Kevin, you make everything so complicated for yourself – hiding in Italy, hiding out here, making everybody suspicious ...
Kevin:	I just want to do the right thing ...
John:	And you do it by being straight, by saying what's in your mind, not by running away, not by hiding, but by coming out with things. Ma will understand all that, Da too. Do you want me to tell them for you?
Kevin:	That'd be great, because Ma won't talk to me ...
John:	*(Lightly)* Course she will ...
Kevin:	And Da says he gets pains in his legs every time he looks at me ...
John:	*(Lightly)* Don't mind him ...
Kevin:	... and they're so proud of you ...
John:	Okay, you leave it to me – and they'll be delighted, you'll see. Because this is all good news, great news, and on their anniversary too – and I'm with you one-hundred per cent, one hundred and ten per cent!

(The kitchen door opens. Doris comes in. She is now

46, dressed in the fashion of the day, very lively. When the door is opened, we hear the party-crowd singing Chirpy Chirpy Cheep Cheep)

Doris: John, what are you doing out here – and is no one looking after Granny? (*Opens the door of the dumb-waiter*) And the fire is nearly gone out in the front-room.

John: But Ma, it's roasting in there ...

Doris: It'll be cold later. (*Pulls the rope. Calls up*) Mammy?

John: Okay, I'll bring in a bucket. (*Fills a bucket from the fuel-room, as*)

Kevin: (*Weakly*) It's really going well, Ma, isn't it?

Doris: (*Looking up the dumb-waiter*) Mammy, let go of the rope. Mammy, I can see you holding it, let go of it ... you should be in bed ...

Kevin: Will I go up to her, Ma?

Doris: (*Annoyed*) Kevin, what are you doing out here? Pauline said she wants yourself and Betty to sing *Whispering Hope*.

Kevin: I don't know *Whispering Hope*.

John: (*Annoyed*) You do!

Kevin: I don't.

John: (*Quietly*) You do whether you do or you don't!

Doris: (*Pulling the rope*) Mammy! Let it go!

John: For God's sake, get on her good side!

Doris: (*Calls*) Mammy, if you don't let go of the rope, the tray won't come down. Mammy, let it go! (*Suddenly a rumble as Mammy lets go and the dumb-waiter comes crashing down. Doris jumps out of the way just in time and it hits the bottom. Empty plates, cutlery, cups and saucers crash out onto the floor*)

Doris: (*Furious*) Mammy!

John:	*(Leaves the coal)* Are you all right, Ma?
	(Kevin and John rush to pick up plates, cutlery)
Doris:	Will you stop fussing, both of you. John, you bring in the coal. Kevin, just put those in the sink and go inside and sing *Whispering Hope* with Betty Boylan.
Kevin:	This saucer is cracked, Ma.
Doris:	*(Furious)* Then throw it out and put the rest in the sink and go in and sing *Whispering Hope!*
	(The dumb-waiter suddenly goes up again. Doris runs to it, as)
Doris:	Mammy! Don't do that!
	(It crashes down again)
	(Calls) That's it – I'm going up to you, Mammy.
John:	I'll go, Ma.
Doris:	You bring in the coal, John.
John:	Okay, then I'll go up to Granny – you take it easy – it's your big day, you should be enjoying yourself. Please. Okay, Ma?
Doris:	*(More calm)* All right. Thank you, John.
	(John goes with a bucket of coal. While the door is opened, we hear the party still singing Chirpy Chirpy Cheep Cheep. *John closes the door now. Doris busies herself, ignoring Kevin)*
Doris:	Now ... the cakes should be done now *(Takes a tray of fairy-cakes from the range)* ... In too long, but they'll be grand ... And a jug of water for the orange-squash for Myra Prendergast ... and more tumblers ... and another plate of sand-wiches should do ... *(Begins to make sandwiches now)*
Kevin:	She's probably lonely up there.

Doris: *(Coldly, as she works)* Pardon, Kevin?

Kevin: Granny – she's probably lonely, locked in her room up there.

Doris: *(Busily and barely controlled)* Is she now? And you'd prefer if I let her out, would you? Have her down here running around the house, turning on the taps, tearing the wall-paper off the walls, galloping out the front door in her nightdress, roaring and shouting and flinging her false teeth at the neighbours. And then awake all night, singing her head off and none of us getting a wink of sleep for days on end. Is that what you'd prefer, Kevin? Or maybe you think she should be sent off somewhere, out of her own house for others to look after her?

Kevin: No, I think it's great she's here ...

Doris: It is, Kevin, and she's staying here! She'll be minded and cared for here as she has had to be for the past four years – while others were off, doing God knows what, in the Irish College in Rome.

Kevin: Ma, I know ... (what you've had to do here)

Doris: *(Hard and direct)* And Kevin, what exactly are you doing out here?

Kevin: *(Nervously)* What? Well I was tell ... tell ... telling John ...

Doris: All my friends are in there and Pauline Boylan wants you to sing *Whispering Hope* with her daughter ...

Kevin: I don't know *Whispering Hope*. ...

Doris: *(Angrily)* For years you sang it with Betty, in this house, out in that garden, on the swing out

25

there – or maybe you've forgotten that too – the same as you seem to have forgotten everything else, including your vocation?

(The kitchen door opens. We hear the crowd singing Song Sung Blue. *Pauline Boylan looks in. She is 40, carrying a drink. High-spirited and glamorous. Behind her will come her daughter, Betty – nineteen, good-looking and also high-spirited)*

Pauline: Is this where you're hiding the prodigal son, Doris?

Doris: Not hiding him, Pauline – he's got too shy to face people.

Pauline: My poor Tim, Lord rest him, used always say that boys studying for the priesthood got that way – shy.

Betty: *(Coming in)* Kevin, come on – they're only screaming for us to sing *Whispering Hope.*

Kevin: I know, Betty, but ...

Betty: *(Giddily)* I said I forgot that stupid thing years ago.

Kevin: Yes, that's what I said.

Pauline: *(To Betty)* You've forgotten Jo Stafford and Gordon McCrae singing *Whispering Hope*?

Betty: *(Merrily)* Yes, Mammy, I've forgotten all that. Kevin, we'll go in and sing something modern: Sonny and Cher *I Got You Babe.*

Pauline: What's wrong with Jo Stafford and Gordon McCrae?

Kevin: *(To Betty)* Would you not sing it with John?

Betty: John hasn't a note in his head.

Doris: *(To Kevin)* Will you go in and stop making excuses.

Betty: Come on, Kevin ... John can listen. *(Suddenly)* Oh Christ!

(John has come in and grabbed Betty around the waist)

John: Who's been talking about me?

Betty: John – you gave me the fright of my life – Kevin and I are going in to do *I Got You Babe*.

John: You better do something – they're roaring for you.

Kevin: But I don't know all the words ...

Betty: Will you stop worrying and come on. *(Goes)*

John: *(Pointed. To Kevin)* Go on – I'll have a chat with Ma here.

Kevin: What? *(Realises)* Oh right. Thanks. *(Goes)*

Pauline: *(Calls)* Or do Jo Stafford and Gordon McCrae ... *(To Doris)* And then, Doris, come in and hear me giving them *(Sings)* 'I have often walked down the streets before ...' *(Goes)*

Doris: *(Calls merrily)* I wouldn't miss that, Pauline – don't start till I get there.

(Doris closes the kitchen door, cutting off the singing of Song Song Blue. *She now continues making sandwiches, as)*

Doris: How's Mammy – is she back in bed?

John: She's grand – asleep now, after she had a good give-out about everything.

Doris: I can imagine – about her ungrateful daughter waiting to grab her lovely house for herself 'and the postman'.

John: None of that, Ma. I told her a few stories – ones I tell the kids at school and she settled back and fell asleep.

27

Doris:	Good. We'll put the kettle on, in case – then we'll bring this stuff in. *(Then, seriously)* And I'm saying nothing, John, but when you and Betty decide to name the day ...
John:	*(Lightly)* You'll be the first to know, Ma.
Doris:	Thank you, John – but remember that this is a big house, with plenty of room ...
John:	Ma ...
Doris:	*(Directly)* And, John, I'd like to keep it in the family – the old house – from my Gran, to my mother, now to me, then on to you. That's important, John.
John:	I know it is, Ma – but that's for another day. Today is for celebrations, for you to enjoy yourself ...
Doris:	Yes and I am. And it could have been so much better if Kevin had only ...
John:	Ma, I wanted to have a word about that.
Doris:	*(Sadly)* It could have been the way it was at Christmas – him home from Rome, in his collar, saying the Grace, giving out the Rosary, talking to everyone, instead of ...
John:	And Ma, there's a chance that we could be back to that.
Doris:	Deed there's not.
John:	No, Kevin was talking to me, telling me something that he wanted to say to you.
Doris:	Well I don't want to hear it, not today.
John:	No, Ma, it's good news – about someone who's coming to talk to you and to him about everything.
Doris:	Pardon?

John: She's a nun, a special nun, coming over here to-day to talk to him, and to you and Da, and she's coming all the way from Rome.

(Doris drops a pan she's holding. She ignores it)

Doris: A nun? Here? From Rome? When?

John: Today, she's at the airport about now – Kevin said she's been sent over specially to see us all … she was supposed to come tomorrow, but now she's here today.

Doris: Today? And why wasn't I told … and what's she seeing us about …

John: About Kevin – it's because they all know he's still very unsure – all this hiding, not contacting us, not talking to anyone …

Doris: Oh my God …

John: And this nun has been sent over to talk to him about all of that, and his vocation, to see what he really thinks.

Doris: Oh thanks be to God.

John: But don't get your hopes up too much, Ma, be-cause I think he's terrified in case she convinces him he should go back and then he leaves again and has to come home again.

Doris: *(Enthusiastic)* No, no, he wouldn't leave again – if he went back he'd never leave again.

John: No, Ma, he might.

Doris: No, no, he always wanted to be a priest – do you remember him as an altar-boy, in his surplice and soutane, bringing home the incense from Benediction and learning the Latin and pretend-ing to say Mass at this very table – *Ad Deum qui laetificat juventutem meam.*

29

John: Well whether or not, Ma, that's what he's been wanting to tell you since he arrived back ...

Doris: God, and we wouldn't listen to him. *(Suddenly)* And where'll she want to stay, this nun – here or in a convent? We'll give her the back room, I'll make up the bed.

John: Ma, do nothing until you talk to Kevin – and don't panic him, he's bad enough as it is.

Doris: Yes. *(Hopefully)* Oh God, John.

(The door opens – and beyond we hear the party singing The Street Where you Live – *and Dan comes in. He is now 47, holding a glass of stout, wearing a party hat. He is very lively, slightly merry. He closes the door)*

Dan: Doris, where's the jug for the orange squash? – Myra Prendergast's tongue is out on her chest, to just above her pioneer pin.

Doris: I forgot all about her.

John: I'll bring it in ...

Doris: No, you stay here for a minute, John.

Dan: *(Filling a jug of water)* And Jack Cunningham is drinking his whiskey neat – I'll top him up before he disgraces us all ... and Sarah Twinkletoes Williamson wants to teach everyone how to do the Slow Twist.

Doris: Dan ...

Dan: And then we're playing snap-apple, soon as I get some apples from the garden – anything to stop Pauline Boylan going on about Jo Stafford and Gordon McCrae. And, Doris, there's special requests for my recitation of *The One-Eyed Yellow Idol to the North of Khatmandu* so I may oblige with that, bring a bit of culture to the proceedings ...

Doris: Dan ...

Dan: ... but I'll have to rehearse it first – and Doris, look *(kicks out his leg)*, not a twinge of pain – as good as Frankie Vaughan. Right, all back inside – cakes and sandwiches first, and then I'll come back and get the apples ...

Doris: *(Hard)* Dan, will you stop and listen to me ...

Dan: But the party's flying – we have to keep it going.

Doris: John has news for us, Dan.

Dan: What? *(Goes to John, hand out, delighted)* Ah son, I couldn't be happier for yourself and Betty ...

John: No, Da, it's not about me or about Betty.

Doris: It's about Kevin.

Dan: Oh Christ – what's that ya-hoo done now?

Doris: He's done nothing ...

John: It's not bad news, Da.

Dan: *(Feels his knee)* Everything about that fellow is bad news ...

Doris: No, Dan ...

Dan: *(Mimics)* 'I want to be a Christian Brother, I don't want to be a Christian Brother; I want to be a priest, I don't want to be a priest ...'

John: No, Da, this news is different.

Doris: This is news about a nun.

Dan: Jaysas, don't tell me he now wants to be a nun!

John: No, Da, a nun has been sent over from Rome to talk him back into being a priest ...

Doris: *(Quickly)* ... and she's arriving today to discuss it all with him ...

John: *(Quickly)* ... and she wants to see you and Ma as well ...

Doris: ... and we're putting her in the back bedroom where it's nice and quiet ...

John: ... or in a convent but Ma says if he goes back to Rome he'll surely stay ...

Doris: And he will, Dan – remember at that table: *Ad Deum qui laetificat juventutem meam.*

Dan: Doris, are you talking in tongues or what?

Doris: No, remember him saying Mass ...

Dan: *(Angrily)* No, I remember nothing, Doris, because today is a day for me to enjoy myself, for my legs to enjoy themselves, and now I'm going back inside ...

Doris: *(Hard)* Dan, stay here! John, you bring that water in for Mrs Prendergast's orange squash ...

John: But Ma ...

Doris: *(A command)* Now, John!

John: Right, Ma.

(John quickly goes. Dan feels his knees)

Doris: Now listen Dan, this is really great news about Kevin ...

Dan: No, Doris, it is not great news – nothing about that fellow is great news: all his life he's had us like headless chickens, not knowing what he was going to do next ...

Doris: No, Dan, he was always sure he wanted to be a priest.

Dan: *(Loudly)* He was never sure about anything! Even out in that garden playing cowboys, he was never sure whether he wanted to be a cowboy or an Indian ... or, let's face it, Doris, a bloody squaw!

Doris:	*(Annoyed)* Dan, don't you ever say ...
Dan:	*(Louder)* It's true, Doris – why couldn't he be like John? – he made up his mind what he wanted to be and he did it and he stuck with it – but that namby-pamby, even in there now, singing *I Got You Babe* with Betty, anyone could see he couldn't make up his mind whether he wanted to be Sonny or bloody Cher! *(The kitchen door has opened. It is Pauline. She has clearly heard Dan shouting)*
Pauline:	Hello? Is there anything wrong?
Dan:	*(Quietly)* Christ!
Doris:	Oh Pauline – no – come in, come in.
Pauline:	I thought I heard somebody shouting.
Doris:	No, that was just Dan ... he was practising ... practising the poem he's going to recite ...
Dan:	*(Roars angrily at Pauline)* 'There's a one-eyed Yellow Idol to the North of Khatmandu, there's a little marble cross below the town: And a broken-hearted woman tends the grave of Mad Carew, while the Yellow God forever gazes down.'
Pauline:	Lovely. And it's a grand party, Doris. I was remembering your wedding day and me in there with Tim, Lord rest him, listening to your mother singing *Bless This House*.
Doris:	Oh, she loved *Bless This House*..
Pauline:	She used to sing it at the top of her voice.
Dan:	*(Coldly)* She still does – usually at about half-three in the morning.
Pauline:	Lovely. And I remember me beside you Doris, as your bridesmaid, you in white, me in pink,

	(*Sadly*) and it's times like this that I really miss Tim ...
Doris:	Ah Pauline, haven't you now got Cyril McBride.
Pauline:	(*Sharply*) Cyril McBride is just for companionship, Doris – no one could ever take the place of poor Tim. (*Sadly*) I can still see him sitting in that room and me, holding his hand, smiling at him, and your Mammy: (*Sings*) 'Bless this house oh Lord we pray ...'
Dan:	(*Can take no more. Roars*) 'There's a one-eyed yellow idol to the North of Khatmandu, there's a little marble cross below the town ...'
Pauline:	Oh, I'll let you get back to it so ... (*Going*)
Doris:	And would you ever take these sandwiches in, Pauline ...
Pauline:	And will I tell them you're on your way?
Doris:	Do, Pauline and thanks.
	(*Pauline goes with the sandwiches*)
Dan:	Bloody gas-bag – that one should've been muzzled at birth.
Doris:	She'll hear you!
Dan:	Tim not cold in the ground and she's off again. That one won't be happy until she's taken poor Cyril McBride's name as well as his freedom.
Doris:	Come on, we'll go in – and you remember what I said about the nun and, when she gets here, listen to her and what she has to say.
Dan:	I think you'll have to rub something into this leg, Doris.
Doris:	(*Gently*) You're not listening to me at all, are you?
Dan:	(*Gently*) Been listening to you for twenty-five

34

	years, haven't I – is that not enough?
Doris:	*(Warmly)* Getting fed-up, are you?
Dan:	Fed-up? *(Lovingly)* Why don't you give this oul leg a rub and see how fed-up I am.
	(They embrace – but suddenly the dumb-waiter goes up and crashes down again)
Doris:	*(Startled)* Mammy! What are you doing?
Dan:	Jesus, that woman!
Doris:	It's all right, Dan – she must want something. *(Goes to the dumb-waiter)*
Dan:	She does – a good boot in the arse.
Doris:	*(Calls up)* Mammy, are you all right?
	(The dumb-waiter crashes again. Doris calls up) All right, Mammy, all right – I'm coming. *(Doris hurries out the kitchen door. Dan goes to the dumb-waiter)*
Dan:	*(Loud and hard)* Get back into bed, you oul hag – a man can't have a minute of privacy with his wife, night or day, with your roaring and interfering ...
	(The dumb-waiter crashes down again, in response)
Dan:	*(Roars)* Yes, go on, object all you like about the bloody postman not being good enough for your daughter with her upbringing and her education – but we're still together, still married, still happy, despite all your sneering about me and my ...
	(The kitchen door opens. Aware of someone coming in, continues in the same tone) '... one-eyed Yellow Idol to the North of Khatmandu, there's a little marble cross ...' *(Sees that it is Kevin. Now normally)*. Oh, it's you – the bloody Phantom of the

	Opera.
Kevin:	*(Nervously)* Hello, Da.
Dan:	I hear the latest is that you're thinking of heading *back* to Rome.
Kevin:	Is ... is that what John told you?
Dan:	Why Kevin, is it a joke? – because your mother certainly believes it, in case you haven't noticed.
Kevin:	*(Upbeat)* Oh, I have – I just met her in the hall and she gave me a big hug and a kiss ...
Dan:	Well congratulations – that's more than I get anymore. *(Then)* And what's this about a nun coming?
Kevin:	Pardon?
Dan:	*(Rubs his knees)* Kevin, for once in your life, can we have straight answers here? Is there a nun coming to this house today or not?
Kevin:	Oh yes, there is.
Dan:	Good. And what will she be saying to us – this nun?
Kevin:	I don't think she'll be saying anything, Da.
Dan:	Why not? – is she a dummy?
Kevin:	No – but she can't speak English.
Dan:	What?
Kevin:	She only speaks Italian. She's an Italian.
Dan:	Then how'll we all know what the hell she's talking to us about?
Kevin:	You won't, but I will – I can speak enough Italian and Latin.
Dan:	Then why does she want to see us?
Kevin:	*(Nervously)* Why, did John say that I said that she wants to see you?
Dan:	*(Barely controlled)* Kevin, do you remember the

	day you sat at that table, after I discovered that somebody had licked all the gum off thirty sheets of stamps that I had left there ... ?
Kevin:	I was only about eight then, Da.
Dan:	... and try as I may, I couldn't get a straight answer out of you ...
Kevin:	I didn't want to annoy you.
Dan:	... and I hit you such a clatter across the head that you swallowed the bundle of stamps you had hidden in your gob – do you remember that?
Kevin:	Yes, Da.
Dan:	*(Calmly)* Well, if I stay here a minute longer, as sure as God, I'll do the same – and then, back in Rome, they'll be ordaining the first priest with a permanent black eye.
Kevin:	Da, all I'm trying to do is ...
Dan:	Now, if anyone is looking for me, I'm out in the back picking apples – if I'm not lying in a heap somewhere, with the legs after going from under me.
Kevin:	Da ... ?
Dan:	Oh, don't worry about me – nobody else bloody-well does.
	(Dan goes into the back garden. Kevin watches him go, concerned. Doris' voice is heard down the dumb-waiter)
Doris:	*(Off)* Dan? Are you there, Dan?
Kevin:	*(Up the dumb-waiter)* He's in the garden, Ma.
Doris:	*(Very caring)* Ah Kevin, love – would you mind sending up a fresh packet of Complan – it's in the top press – Granny has destroyed this one.

37

Kevin: Complan. Okay Ma.

(As Kevin gets this, Betty comes in the kitchen door, somewhat uneasily. She has a glass of Bacardi and a packet of cigarettes. Beyond we can hear the party singing Make Me an Island)

Betty: *(Quietly)* Hi.

Kevin: Oh, hello. Just getting some Complan for Granny.

Betty: *(Whispers)* Okay. *(Closes the kitchen door).*

Kevin: *(Calls up)* Coming up, Ma. *(Pulls up the rope).*

Doris: *(Off)* Thanks Kevin – now you don't be staying down there on your own – go back inside and enjoy yourself and don't be worrying.

Kevin: *(Calls)* Okay Ma. *(Then, to Betty)* Gone.

Betty: Good. *(Then)* Just popped in to drink this in peace ... and to say that I really enjoyed that.

Kevin: What, me and Ma?

Betty: No, you and me, inside. Sonny and Cher.

Kevin: *(Awkwardly)* Oh yes. I didn't think I'd remember the words, but I did.

Betty: *(Sings)* 'I got you babe'. *(Awkwardly)* Better, any day, than that oul *Whispering Hope.* Just because we used to sing it on the swing out there.

Kevin: *(Amused)* Yeah ... *(Sings)* 'Whispering Soap, oh Whispering Rope ...'

Betty: *(Joining in)* ... 'Oh Whispering Pope, oh Whispering dope' – your mother used to hate us making a laugh of it.

Kevin: Yeah. *(Imitates with Betty)* 'Sing it right or don't sing it at all.'

Betty: Yes. *(Then)* And I'm really sorry it didn't work out for you in Rome and everything – sorry, but not too surprised. Always said you were too good for that.

Kevin: What? Oh, right. Thanks. *(To tell her)* Well, as a matter of fact ...

Betty: *(Continuing)* ... and I don't mind telling you this, Kevin – well, I do mind really, but this Bacardi helps – but I was really ... disappointed ... when I heard you were going away.

Kevin: Betty ...

Betty: *(Backing down)* Oh, don't worry – not because I fancied you or anything – I didn't, I don't, even if everybody always thought I did, I didn't and I still don't – but I was, you know, disappointed, all the same. *(Quickly)* Cigarette?

Kevin: What? *(Considers)* Eh ... no thanks. Matches here somewhere. *(Finds them. Lights her cigarette, as)* Never saw you smoking before.

Betty: Oh, I quite enjoy cigarettes now. And the occasional Bacardi. *(Moves closer)*

Kevin: *(Moves nervously away)* Oh, good. And you and John are getting along all right, are you?
(Betty goes and turns the key in the kitchen door)

Betty: *(By explanation).* Just in case Mammy wanders in, sees me on the booze and has a fit. But John? *(Drinks)* Let's just say that John has a full life.

Kevin: Has he?

Betty: Oh yes: the school, the homework, the grinds, PTA meetings, staff meetings and now, with his post of responsibility, you can add on football, basketball, volley-ball and that's when he's not here with your Mammy, your Granny, your family, all that.

Kevin: Oh right.

Betty: And somewhere in there is me. *(Of the cigarette)* Would you like a drag?

Kevin: Pardon? Oh no ... *(Then)* Well maybe I ... *(Almost decides. Then nervously moves away).* No. No, I won't, thank you.

Betty: *(Amused)* It's only a cigarette, Kevin – no need to run away from it.

Kevin: *(Moving away)* Yes, I know what it is ... and I'm not ... just ... no thanks.

Betty: You don't mind me asking you something, do you?

Kevin: What? Well no, not really ...

Betty: You do still like girls, don't you?

Kevin: Pardon me?

Betty: *(Lightly)* No, I mean, since Rome and those priests and everything, you might have discovered that you don't really like girls anymore and that now you might be ... you know ... ?

Kevin: *(Angrily)* Betty, I think you better explain what exactly you mean by ...

(Betty has suddenly seen Dan arrive at the back door. He carries a few apples)

Betty: *(Panic)* Oh my God – here's your Da! Quick, hold that. *(Gives Kevin her cigarette)*

Kevin: What? No, I can't ...

(Dan is already in. Kevin has taken the cigarette and now hides it behind his back. Betty puts her drink aside)

Dan: Well, well, what's this? Rehearsing another Sonny and Cher number in here, are you?

Betty: No, no, just talking. Weren't we, Kevin?

Kevin: What? Yes, just talking, Da, that's all.

Dan: *(To Kevin)* And smoking.

Kevin: Pardon?

Dan: *(Patiently)* Are you also smoking a cigarette?

Kevin: Me? No. *(The rising smoke is obvious)* Oh, do you mean this cigarette? *(Shows it now)*

Dan: That's the one. Smoking that, are you?

Kevin: What? *(Bravely)* Yes, I was. I am. *(More courageously, for Betty's benefit)* I do smoke a bit now, Da. In fact, I quite enjoy it.

Dan: Do you? And do you also 'quite enjoy' wearing lipstick?

Kevin: Pardon?

Dan: That's lipstick, isn't it? – on your cigarette?

Kevin: What? Oh, no, no ...

Betty: Yes, it is, Mr Gillespie, that's mine, that's my lipstick. Kevin gave me a pull.

Kevin: *(By explanation)* Of the cigarette. *(Dan looks at him)* That ... that's how it got there – the li ... li ... lipstick. *(Stubs it out)*

Dan: I see. Well I'll leave you to it. *(Tries to open the door. Locked. More angry)* You don't mind if I unlock this door, do you?

Kevin: No, no, we only locked it because ... because ... because ... *(Looks to Betty. No help)* by mistake.

Dan: Betty, you don't speak Italian, do you?

Betty: Italian? No.

Dan: Pity. You could have helped us understand what the hell is going on here today.

(Dan goes. Betty is amused, picks up her drink. Kevin upset)

Betty: What did he mean by that – speaking Italian?

Kevin: *(Angrily)* What did you mean by handing me

that cigarette and saying nothing when he asked you who locked the door ...

Betty: *(Laughs)* And the lipstick – I could have screamed!

Kevin: ... and asking me that stupid, bloody question just as he was ...

Betty: *(Amused)* About you liking girls?

Kevin: *(Furious)* Yes, about me liking girls – why the hell shouldn't I like girls?

Betty: For God's sake, Kevin, calm down – I was only joking.

Kevin: *(Stops)* What?

Betty: I was only getting it up for you – why else would I say it? *(Then)* Don't I remember Glendalough, the day you and I went there in that funny bus?

Kevin: What? *(To diminish)* No, no, that wasn't just you and me, there was a whole crowd of us ...

Betty: But I was the only one you asked to climb with you up to Kevin's Bed ...

Kevin: What?

Betty: St Kevin's Bed, the cave in Glendalough – you said we should climb up to it because it had your name ... *(Then, teasing)* but we know that wasn't your only reason, don't we?

Kevin: Betty, this was nearly four years ago – I was only eighteen.

Betty: I was only sixteen – and I have more reasons to forget it than you.

Kevin: For God's sake, nothing happened in Kevin's Bed.

Betty: Don't I know it – didn't I nearly get hysterical

42

	when you tried to put your hand near me ...
Kevin:	No, no, I wasn't going to do anything ...
Betty:	I didn't give you much chance, did I? *(Pointed)* ... but you did want me, Kevin, didn't you?
Kevin:	Betty, listen ...
Betty:	*(Annoyed)* I know, I know, and now there's John, my fiance – no need to keep reminding me! *(Then)* But while we're here, we really should celebrate your return, Kevin – your coming back to the real world ... *(Goes to him)*
Kevin:	Betty, please – I have to tell you ...
Betty:	Shush. Tell me nothing. Blame it all on the Bacardi. *(Arms around his neck)* Think of Kevin's Bed – and how stupid I was then ... and how I've changed now.
Kevin:	*(Resisting a little)* Betty ...
	(Betty kisses Kevin. He begins to respond. Then the kitchen door opens and John walks in. Kevin leaps back)
Betty:	*(Angrily)* For God's sake, who unlocked that door?
Kevin:	Sorry, John, we were just ... Betty just came in to ...
John:	*(Controlled)* It's okay, Kevin, it's okay. Betty, I think you should go inside.
Betty:	*(Angrily)* I beg your pardon?
John:	*(More angry)* You heard me, Betty – I said you should go inside – and now!
Betty:	I'm sorry, John, but this isn't your school – I'm not one of your pupils ...
John:	... and stop drinking that bloody Bacardi ...
Betty:	Or what? I'll get detention, be told to stand out

	to the line ... ?
John:	No – you'll end up making an even bigger fool of yourself.
Betty:	*(To Kevin)* You see, Kevin, John's far to aware of his position to approve of me welcoming you back.
John:	Betty, what I don't approve of is you making yourself the laughing stock of ...
Betty:	*(Angrily)* You don't approve of much, John, do you?
Kevin:	*(Upset)* Please ...
John:	*(More angry)* Well I certainly don't approve of you carrying on with someone who is about to become a priest.
Betty:	Maybe I should carry on with you then?
John:	Well that certainly would be more fitting ...
Betty:	*(Angrily)* Yes, more fitting if I could get near you with all your bloody rules and regulations about what we can do and what we can't do ... *(To Kevin)* in case the parents from the school might see us and what they might think of him ...
John:	Betty, you stop this now!
Betty:	*(Furiously to John)* ... and when it's not that, it's 'we have to be careful' or 'wait till we're married' – well, for God's sake, let's *get* married or let's take an oath to be careful but, for Christ sake, let's do something! *(Silence)*
John:	*(Calmly)* Well, now that you've got that off your chest ...
Betty:	*(Quietly to John)* Long time waiting for *you* to

	get anything off my chest.
John:	... it may help you sober up to know that all this is a waste of time, that Kevin won't be around much longer, that he's returning to Rome to finish his studies for the priesthood ...
Betty:	Nice try, John.
John:	He'll tell you himself that there's a clerical counsellor coming here to talk to him today. *(To Kevin)* Kevin?
Kevin:	Well ... eh ... yes, Betty – but I need time to ...
Betty:	What?
John:	Yes, Betty – suddenly makes you feel a bit stupid, doesn't it?
Betty:	*(To Kevin)* And you let me go on about ... ?
Kevin:	No I didn't, all the time I was trying to ...
Betty:	*(Seething with rage)* You know what your trouble is, both of you – you think you're wonderful, God's gift to the world, Butch Cassidy and the Sundance Kid – but you're just two spineless bastards and no woman should be let within a mile of either of you: one afraid to do anything because of what people might think, and the other running away because deep down he doesn't like girls ... *(To Kevin)* and I meant what I said about you, Kevin, so forget Kevin's Bed and what happened there and off you go, back to Rome and stay there with all the other men and all the altar boys and see if I care!
	(Betty storms out. Silence. Then)
John:	*(Awkwardly)* Don't mind that – that's just the Bacardi talking.
Kevin:	*(Awkwardly)* Oh, I know ...

John:	She'll be full of apologies later ...
Kevin:	Of course.
John:	Betty doesn't often drink – but when she does she comes out with the most awful rubbish ... about me and her and ...
Kevin:	No, no, I know – and what she said about me ...
John:	Oh, I know – rubbish. Once she sobers up, she won't even remember it.
Kevin:	Absolutely.
John:	*(Then, concerned)* But what she said about you and her ... in your bed or something ...
Kevin:	No, no, that was Kevin's Bed, in Glendalough ...
John:	*(Relieved)* Oh, Glendalough? Right, that's what I thought. Yes, she won't remember a thing, so best just let it pass.
	(The door opens and Doris comes in. Very excited. She will now try to tidy the kitchen as)
Doris:	Kevin, Kevin, she's coming, she's here.
Kevin:	Who?
Doris:	The nun. *(Kisses Kevin)* And I'm so delighted, love, and no pressure on you at all, but please God now. Oh, will you look at this kitchen.
John:	Calm down, Ma.
Kevin:	Where is she, Ma?
Doris:	In a taxi, just pulled up outside, and she has a suitcase, so she must be staying ...
Kevin:	Oh my God ...
Doris:	It's all right, Kevin, no one else knows, except your father, he's keeping the sing-song going. What does a nun have in her room? *(Takes down the statue)* I'll move the Child of Prague in there – and John, clear those cups away and don't be

standing looking at me.

John: But Ma, she won't be coming in here ...

Doris: She will so – I'm not having her meeting every-body first thing – I'll bring her around the back and in this way ...

Kevin: Or Ma, maybe I can have a word with her first? (*The dumb-waiter rattles*)

Doris: (*Calls*) Oh, Mammy, not now – the nun is coming.

Kevin: I thought we were telling nobody?

Doris: And who can Mammy tell, up there in her room?

(*The kitchen door opens. Pauline comes in. Beyond, we can hear a lively rendition of* Seven Drunken Nights)

Pauline: Doris the nun is coming up the garden path.

Kevin: Ma, I thought nobody knew.

Doris: But Pauline is almost family.

Pauline: Kevin, why isn't she dressed like a nun?

Doris: Since Vatican Two they don't have to, Pauline – and now, will you go and make sure no one opens the door to her until I do – and tell Dan to stop singing that filthy *Seven Drunken Nights* ...

Pauline: All right. And Kevin, I'm going to ask her to sing *Panis Angelicus* – nuns sing that lovely. (*Goes, closing the door*)

Kevin: For God's sake, she's not here for a sing-song.

John: (*To Kevin*) Will you relax – calm down. (*The door-bell rings*)

Kevin: There she is. I'll go ...

Doris: No you will not, Kevin – I will let her in and bring her around and you be here to meet her.

	And you stay here too, John – and your father can stay inside, so you won't be upset, Kevin. *(Quietly)* Please God now, please God.
Kevin:	But Ma ... *(As Doris goes)* Ma ...! *(She has gone, closing the kitchen door)*
John:	*(To Kevin)* Just take it nice and easy.
Kevin:	*(Nervously)* Right, and John, I might try to have a private word in Italian with her ... before she ... before anyone ...
John:	*(Lightly)* You'll be able to have a million private words with her in any language you like – so just relax. And remember, I'm with you one hundred and ten per cent.
Kevin:	Great, but if I could just see her before anyone ...
John:	And this looks like them.
	(Doris has come in the back door. She carries a suitcase. Behind her is a 20 year old Italian woman, Maria)
Doris:	*(Excited)* Hello, now this is Sister Maria – I'm afraid I haven't been able to understand a single word, except her name. *(To Maria)* Sister, this is my son John – and, of course, Kevin.
	(Maria goes to Kevin. Puts her hands to his face)
Maria:	*(Sincerely)* Ciao Kevin, che bello rivederti.
	(The dumb-waiter suddenly crashes down. Maria jumps, looking at it. Doris tries to reassure her with a smile and a gesture ... as we quickly fade to darkness)

END OF SCENE ONE, ACT ONE

Note: an appendix of Italian translation is at the back of this book on pp. 122.

ACT ONE

SCENE TWO

Lights Up. It is present-day again. Therefore, the kitchen is as it was at the beginning of the play – again with its abnormal light-ing and darkness beyond the kitchen window. The dumb-waiter door is closed. Kevin is alone in the room, remembering. His tie is done-up and he wears his glasses. He is 47 again.

Now, in his memory, he hears voices from long ago: Two children singing Whispering Hope.

Through the window, he (and we) now see the young boy and girl, in the apple tree garden, in summer, in beautiful light – she on the swing, he pushing it, both happily singing the song.

[If, in production, the presence of the boy and girl presents a difficulty, this flashback will work with just a moving, empty swing and the voices of the children. However, if possible, their actual presence is preferred.]

Kevin watches, remembering. Establish. Then, we begin to hear the party lustily singing Arrivederci Roma. *The garden/children fades as the party sounds dominate. The light in the kitchen changes and we are back to the Silver Anniversary. Kevin has his tie pulled loose and has removed his glasses. He is 22 again.*

The kitchen door opens and we hear, clearly, the crowd singing Arrivederci Roma *as John stands, angrily looking at Kevin. He carries some used glasses for washing.*

John:	Jesus Christ, do you have some questions to answer!
Kevin:	*(Nervously)* Why, what's happening in there?
John:	*(Closes the door. Goes to the sink)* Oh, everything's

	great 'in there' – Sister Maria is a great hit, Ma delighted to have *A* Nun in the house while *The* Nun is sitting there singing *Arrivederci Roma* with Betty on the piano ...
Kevin:	And is Betty all right? Did she say anything else about ... ?
John:	Betty is grand, Betty is sober, Betty forgets – but what about the other one – what the hell is she, Kevin?
Kevin:	Who?
John:	Sister shaggin Maria – and I want this straight and I want it now – is she really a nun, like a real nun, is she?
Kevin:	Why, did she say she isn't?
John:	No one knows what the blazes she's saying – she's talking non-stop gobbledegook in there ...
Kevin:	Then that's all right – because I got the chance to talk to her privately, in Italian, and I told her to be a nun, so Ma won't be worried and Da won't be annoyed and the anniversary won't be spoiled and ...
John:	'To be a nun'? So she's not a nun?
Kevin:	What?
John:	Kevin, do I have to beat the shit out of you before you ... (tell me)
Kevin:	*(Angrily).* No, all right, no she isn't a nun but ...
John:	But you swore to me ... you stood there and distinctly told me ...
Kevin:	*(Angrily)* But I had to say that because you shouted at me and I knew that everyone would have been shouting and if only she came tomorrow but she couldn't get a flight tomorrow

	and I couldn't stop her because she's very strong-willed and ...
John:	So what is she? She's not a mot, is she?
Kevin:	Why does everyone assume ... ?
John:	All right, don't tell me – but any minute they'll all be out here and if I'm not on your side ...
Kevin:	All right, yes, she is, she is ... well sort of ... okay, she's just someone I met when I went to Naples for a holiday – I went with Tadgh Quinlan, another seminarian – and all I did was just speak to her and since then she's never left me alone – phone calls and letters and she got my address from Tadgh – and she insisted on coming but, the thing is, she'll be gone soon, tomorrow, and no one need ever ...
John:	Jesus Christ.
Kevin:	But when I realised that I couldn't put her off, I had to make up this nun thing as quick as I could because Ma loves nuns and I couldn't say she was just a woman or Ma ...
John:	Jesus, what is it about you and women? Betty fancies you, this one is chasing you half-way across Europe ...
Kevin:	No, I only met her in Naples – her father has a vineyard there and they make their own wine and ...
John:	I don't give a shite about her father or his wine – what is all this going to do to Ma and Da? How's all this going to sound down at the school? Do you ever think of that? Christ! *(Now more calm)* Okay, okay, we'll stick to the nun story for now – she's a nun and she comes from

Rome, not Naples.

Kevin: Not Naples, right. And the thing is, if we just get through today – to be honest, Maria is not too happy about being a nun but she'll go along with it and that'll keep everybody happy.

John: *(Hard)* And what about tomorrow, Kevin – do you ever think about tomorrow?

(Pauline comes in, carrying crockery. She is followed by Doris, carrying more. From now, with each arrival, a spate of washing and drying. Party sounds from beyond, when the door is open)

Pauline: *(As she comes)* No, Doris, we'll have these done in no time.

Doris: *(As she comes)* Leave them, Pauline – we're going to play cards soon.

Pauline: No, no, we'll wash them and then we'll be done with it.

Doris: Ah Kevin, you're missing Sister Maria's lovely singing.

Pauline: Kevin will soon be hearing it all again in Rome.

Doris: John, tell Pauline to go in and start the cards.

John: Yes, Mrs Boylan, we'll do these here.

Pauline: *(At the sink)* No, no, many hands. *(As she works)* And isn't it a shame that Sister Maria hasn't a word of English.

Doris: *(At the sink)* Though did you hear Larry Heffernan say that most Italians can only speak Italian.

Pauline: And what about Pope Paul?

Doris: Oh, Pope Paul is different – at Christmas, in his *Urbi et Orbi*, didn't he even speak in Irish?

Pauline: I could have cried when I heard him. And Kevin, Sister Maria doesn't know *Panis Angelicus*.

John:	*(Quickly)* Didn't she give you *Arrivederci Roma*?
Pauline:	God, that was lovely – it'd make you want to pack your bags and leave for Rome today.
John:	*(Lightly)* Except that it means goodbye to Rome.
Pauline:	What matter what it means. And, Kevin, what part of Italy is she from – Sister Maria.
Kevin:	*(Quickly)* Not Naples.
John:	Christ!
Kevin:	I mean Rome – she's from Rome.
Pauline:	Rome. As my poor Tim used to always say 'The Infernal City'.
	(General laughter as Dan comes in, carrying more dishes)
Dan:	Here's a few more ...
Doris:	Dan, you go in and get the cards going ...
Dan:	I think Sarah Twinkle-toes is going to do a bit of flamenco dancing for Sister Maria. She said if they don't do it in Italy, they ought to.
	(Betty comes in with more plates. She is in good form – clearly having made up with John)
Betty:	Mammy, you're to go in – Annie O'Driscoll wants to sing a duet with you.
Pauline:	Not after you singing with Sister.
John:	Yes, you were wonderful.
Betty:	It was her – the Singing Nun eat your heart out.
Doris:	*(Remembering)* The Singing Nun! What was it?
Doris/Pauline:	*(Merrily sing)* 'Domineque, a neque, a neque-a ...'
	(They try to sing on, as)
John:	*(To Betty)* Are you all right, love?
Betty:	*(Kisses him)* I'm great.
Doris:	Isn't she lovely-looking too – for a nun, that is.

53

John: *(Lightly)* And why shouldn't nuns be lovely-looking, Ma?

Doris: No, I mean young-looking.

Kevin: *(Quickly)* She joined up when she was fourteen. *(All look to Kevin)*

John: *(To cover)* They do that in Italy – join up young.

Pauline: The only thing I'm disappointed in is, of all the songs she knows she doesn't know ...

Dan/Pauline/Doris/Betty: *Panis Angelicus*
(General laughter)

Doris: All I want her to sing – when she is finished talking to Kevin and everything – is *Come Back to Sorrento*. That's one of your favourites, isn't it, Dan?

Dan: Oh, a great song – *Sorrento*.
(Pauline starts and then Doris, Dan, John, Betty join in singing Sorrento. *Then the door opens, Maria appears and all suddenly stop singing)*

Maria: Scusate il disturbo.

Doris: *(In a similar accent)* Ah, Sister, come-a in, come-a in, there-a is something you-a want, yes?

Dan: Jesus, Doris, I didn't know you could speak Italian.

Maria: *(Annoyed and quickly)* Kevin, perche mi lasci con ste persone che credono che io sia una suora; loro non parlano Italiano io non parlo Inglese; tu stai qua con la tua famiglia e quand'e che riusciremo a parlare un po'io e te?

Kevin: Parleremo quando se ne saranno andati tutti.

Maria: *(Angrily)* Ma qui non se ne va nessuno – sono li che cantano e si raccontano storie – non sono certo venuta perche io e te potessimo stare insieme.

54

Doris: Kevin, does Sister want the toilet? *(To Maria in an accent)* Toileta? Lav-a-tory?

Kevin: *(Annoyed)* It's all right Ma. *(To Maria)* Parleremo domani e ti spieghero tutto. Oggi, pero, ti prego, tu sei Suor Maria.

Maria: *(Annoyed)* D'accordo, Ma poi mi dovrai spieg-are tutto per filo e per segno. *(To all, kindly)* Scusate il disturbo. Grazie tante, a piu tardi.
(Maria goes. Pause. All look to Kevin)

Kevin: Oh, eh – Sis ... Sis ... Sister Maria was just saying that as this is your wedding anniversary, you should be inside, being happy, enjoying your-selves, and not out here, washing dishes.

Pauline: Well isn't that lovely?

Betty: *(Pointed, to Kevin)* She seemed annoyed to me.

John: *(Defending)* No, no, Italians always seem an-noyed – it's the way they speak. Right, we all heard what she said – so all back in – Ma, Da, Mrs Boylan, Betty ...

Doris: I'll just get more water for Myra Prendergast's orange squash ...

Dan: I'll get it, Doris – you go on in.

Doris: And Kevin, you come inside too ...

Dan: Kevin and I will be in in a minute.

Pauline: *(Going)* Doris, I loved the way you said *(In the accent)* lav-a-tory. Is that the Italian word for it too?

Doris: *(Going. Merrily)* It might be.

John: *(Going)* In France, it's pissoir.

Doris: John! *(Goes)*

John: No, it is! *(Goes)*

Betty: *(Pointedly to Kevin)* Nice young girl – does she

know everything about you? *(Goes)*
(Pauline, Doris, Betty and John are gone, laughing.
The door is closed. Kevin and Dan are left. Silence.
Kevin uneasy)

Kevin: I suppose I'd better go in too.

Dan: *(Rubs his leg)* In a minute.

Kevin: Sorry, Da?

Dan: *(Louder)* I said in a minute! *(Pause. To himself)*
Panis Angelicus! Arriverderci Roma! Come Back to
Sorrento! What next!

Kevin: *(Pause)* I think I really should ... (go)

Dan: *(Angrily)* I said in a minute! Or have you been
timing me – is my minute up or what?

Kevin: No, Da – whatever you say.

Dan: Yes, whatever I say! Well, here's what I say: I
say that, to you with all your education and your
degrees, I may be only some kind of half-wit,
with only enough brains to read envelopes and
push letters into letter boxes.

Kevin: No, Da ...

Dan: *(Harder)* ... but I'm not so thick, I'm not such a
gobshite as to believe that that Sister Maria in
there is a nun. I'm not that dense, Kevin.

Kevin: No, Da, she really is ...

Dan: *(Loudly)* Dressed in civvies, singing and gallaring,
yapping at the top of her voice – what convent
would stick that? If you told me she was really
a chimpanzee, you'd have a better chance of me
believing it. So out with it – plain talking now
Kevin, between the two of us – what is she?

Kevin: All ... all right, Da – she ... she's not really a nu
... nu ... nun. *(Then)* Supposing I just said she

	was a postulant.
Dan:	*(Then)* A prostitute?
Kevin:	No, a postulant – someone who isn't a nun but ...
Dan:	I'm not interested in what she isn't – I want to know what she is. And now, Kevin *(Shouts)* Now!
Kevin:	*(Then)* All right, Da. She ... she ... she's ... a girl ...
Dan:	A girl? Good. Now we're getting somewhere.
Kevin:	... that I met when I was on holidays in ... in Sorrento ... and, after I left Rome, she followed me here.
Dan:	She followed you?
Kevin:	Because ... because I think she likes me.
Dan:	*(Flatly)* She likes you.
Kevin:	I ... I never encouraged her or anything ...
Dan:	So she's not here to get you back to Rome, to the priesthood? She's here for the opposite, in fact.
Kevin:	Yes, Da – but she'll be gone soon – tomorrow – I told her, in Italian, to be Sister Maria for today, and tomorrow I'll explain it all to her and let her go back to Naples ... Rome ... Sorrento, where she came from.
Dan:	*(Calmly)* And does anyone else know about this?
Kevin:	No! *(Then)* Except John – I told John.
Dan:	*(Sadly)* John! And all his talk too about her being a nun.
Kevin:	It's all only so's not to upset Ma. That's why we're doing all this, Da, that's all we're thinking of.
Dan:	*(Controlled fury)* Are you? Well you have a funny way of going about it!
	(The door opens and John comes in. Applause is heard beyond. He closes the door. He carries some used

glasses. In great form)

John: Great gas in there now – you should go in, Da – Sister Maria is going down a bomb.

Kevin: *(Trying to alert him)* John ...

John: Mrs Boylan just asked her again if she'd have a go at *Panis Angelicus,* but instead she gave us three verses of *Volare* and she was terrific. *(Singing* Volare)

Kevin: *(Anxiously)* John ...

Dan: *(Coldly)* Bit unusual to hear nuns singing pop songs, isn't it?

John: Oh no, Da, that's the way nuns are today – ever since the Pope decreed all the changes for the Second Vatican Council.

Dan: *(Suddenly angry)* Is that so? And did the Pope also 'decree' that sons could tell barefaced lies to their father, treat him like a gobshite, a half-wit, a bloody thick?

John: *(Taken aback)* What?

Kevin: I told Da about her not being a nun.

John: What?!

Kevin: Only just now ...

John: *(Furious)* Oh, well thanks very much!

Kevin: I tried to stop you.

John: And who else have you told?

Kevin: No one else – we're the only ones that know.

Dan: *(Angrily)* Yes, and for your sakes, it better stay that way – because if your mother hears about this, it'll kill her.

John: But Da, she won't hear it.

Dan: She better not or, as God is my judge, I'll crack open your skull minutes after I've cracked open

58

his.

John: *(Calmly)* Da, I know, but there's nothing to worry about – no one's going to know.

Dan: They bloody-well better not! *(Calmer to Kevin)* And all right if that young wan has to be here today, if your mother sees nothing wrong with that – all right. But tomorrow, I want her out of here, her bags packed and back to Sorrento, with or without you.

Kevin: She will Da, don't worry.

John: *(To Kevin)* Sorrento?

Kevin: That's where she comes from *(Pointed)*, like in the song, the one that Da likes.

John: *(Quietly)* Jesus Christ – first Naples, then Rome, now Sorrento. Why not Africa, why not the North Pole?!

(The kitchen door opens. We hear the party singing Sloop John B *as Doris comes in)*

Doris: Ah Dan, everyone is inside asking for you and you're all in here.

Dan: *(Moving)* I know, sorry Doris – the lads and myself were having an oul anniversary chat.

Doris: Well have that when everybody's gone, in you go now. And Kevin, you stay here – I have Sister coming out to you.

Dan: She's coming in here? The nun?

Doris: And why wouldn't she? – she's hardly seen Kevin since she arrived and this'll be private ...

Kevin: No, Ma, it's not really necessary ...

Doris: Well of course it's necessary, what else is she here for?

(Maria appears at the kitchen door)

Ah Sister, come in, come in – and the rest of you, inside.

Maria: *(Coming in)* Grazie, grazie mille, Signora.

John: Hello again, Sister. Excuse me, we're going inside.

Maria: Buona sera.

Dan: *(With difficulty)* Excuse me ... Sister.

(Dan and John go)

Doris: Now Sister, I'll leave you here with Kevin. *(In an accent)* With Kev-in. Me go. You stay. And no disturb. Okay.

Maria: Grazie signora.

Doris: Not at all, Sister. And Kevin, no pressure at all, take your time, and no one will come near you, and please God now.

(Doris goes, closing the door. Maria's demeanour immediately changes to one of petulance)

Maria: Kevin, sona venuta fin a qua da Napoli per vederti e tu mi lasci la.

Kevin: *(Not as fluent)* Ti prego! Smettila Maria! Ascoltami, ci sono delle persone qui che sanno che non sei una suora.

Maria: *(Annoyed)* Io non l'ho detto a nessuno!

Kevin: Lo so che ...

Maria: *(Angrily)* ... Mi sono tolta il rossetto, mi sono tolta lo smalto, e sto cantando delle canzoni sceme ...

Kevin: Lo so ...

Maria: *(Angrily)* ... Non lo sapevo che venivo qui a far la parte della suora. Qui io credevo di venirci per essere la tua fidanzata.

Kevin: *(Flattering)* Lo so, e tutto cosi sciocco – perche tu

	sei troppo bella per essere una suora. La gente se ne accorge.
Maria:	*(Gently)* Oh, Kevin – mi dispiace. Lo volevo soltanto che tutto fosse meraviglioso. *(Kisses him. Holds him)* Mi sei mancato cosi tanto.
Kevin:	*(Gently)* Ache tu. Tutto andra per il meglio purche mia madre non lo venga a sapere.
Maria:	*(Concerned)* Tup padre lo sa?
Kevin:	Si – e anche mio fratello John.
Maria:	*(Loving and comforting)* Oh caro, non ti preoccupare. *(Kisses him)*
	(The kitchen door opens. Party sounds are heard. Betty steps in. Kevin and Maria jump apart. Betty closes the door and comes in)
Betty:	*(Coldly)* Excuse me for interrupting. I'm just getting some water for Mr Dempsey.
Kevin:	*(Embarrassed)* Oh. Right. You weren't ... Ma said that no one is supposed to come in while myself and ... sis ... Sister Maria ...
Betty:	*(Sharper)* For God's sake, Kevin, please – don't insult me by still saying that she's a nun.
Kevin:	Well, as a matter of fact ...
Betty:	*(Harder)* Or that you are not one of the greatest bastards on the face of this earth.
Kevin:	What?
Betty:	Or is this just a fling, a little holiday romance, something you need to sort yourself out?
Kevin:	I don't see why it should bother you what I ...
Betty:	*(Hard)* Do you not, Kevin? – well the *why* is that only hours ago, I trusted you enough to tell you how I felt about you ...
Kevin:	Betty, you happen to be engaged to John ...

Betty: Yes and I trusted you enough to tell you that I never *wanted* to get engaged to John ...

Kevin: You never said that!

Betty: *(Upset)* Kevin, you know damn well that if you stayed, I would never ... it was only when you left that I ... the only reason I ever got engaged to John was ...

Maria: *(Louder and quickly)* Kevin, cosa stai dicendo? Non restero ad ascoltarti mentre parli ...

Betty: *(Furiously to Maria)* Oh, shut up for God's sake!

Kevin: *(Hard)* Betty, you have no right to shout at her ...

Betty: *(Emotional)* I have every right – because, Kevin, whether you like it or not, we go back a long time ...

Kevin: We do not!

Betty: *(Upset)* Kevin, we do – we were always together, ask anyone, going across the fields, playing out there, swinging on the swing, up in the apple trees ...

Kevin: Betty, you're drunk ...

Betty: ... and what about the charm bracelet you gave me ...

Kevin: I gave you the charms, not the bracelet ...

Betty: You gave me the heart, you gave me the cherub ... *(Crying)* And what about us in Kevin's Bed ...?

Kevin: Not that again!

Betty: Yes again, Kevin – because you wanted me then, Kevin, you did, you really did! – and John doesn't give a damn about me, it's only the school, the students, the parents, the promotions ...

Kevin: Yes, and now it's me and Maria ...

Betty:	No, it is not Maria ...
Maria:	Che stai dicendo di me?
Betty:	... because it can't be her, Kevin, because I'm not letting you go again ...
Kevin:	*(Loudly)* Will you get it into your head, Betty, you never had me to let go – and you don't have me now.
Betty:	*(Now angrily)* All right okay fine! – then neither will she – because you have changed, you are different from Glendalough, something happened to you after that and you mightn't know what it was ...
Kevin:	Betty ...
Betty:	... but suddenly, for some reason, you don't like girls anymore.
Kevin:	You're talking rubbish ...
Betty:	You don't know what you are but, one thing is certain, you'll never do much with her ...
Maria:	Come hai detto?
Kevin:	Betty, you are drunk ...
Betty:	*(Hard and clear)* ... because if you want my opinion, I'll tell you what you are: you are a homosexual. It's all so obvious, Kevin – that's why you loved Rome, loved being with all those men ...
Kevin:	Betty, if you don't shut-up ...
Betty:	No, I will not shut-up. *(Shouts at Maria)* Did you hear that? Homosexual. Only likes men. Not women ...
Maria:	*(Puzzled)* Cosa sta dicendo quella?
Kevin:	Betty, get out of here ...
Betty:	*(To Maria)* He will never do anything with you.

Homosexual. Him.

Kevin: Stop it, Betty.

Maria: *(Realises. Shouts)* Kevin? No, no, non e assolutamente vero. Non e omosessuale! No!

Betty: Ah, she understands.

Maria: No-no-no-no!

Betty: Yes-yes-yes-yes!

Kevin: ... shut-up ...

Maria: *(Shouts at Betty)* Non e vero perche aspettiamo un bambino.

Betty: *(Not understanding)* You're wasting your time. Go back to Italy ...

Maria: *(Clearly, with signs)* No, no io e Kevin avremo un bambino. Sono incinta. *(In English)* Pregnant!

Kevin: Zitta Maria ...

Maria: *(Indicating)* ... Madre ... Padre ... Bambino. Tuti noi. Una famiglia. Un bambino.

Betty: *(Stunned)* Baby? Bambino? What is she talking about? Kevin! I don't believe this! *(Angrily)* She's pregnant and you're the father?

Kevin: Now Betty, I don't want any of this to get out.

Betty: Oh, you bastard! How could you? Why her? What was wrong with me ... ? *(Suddenly and furiously overturns the table)* You bastard, Kevin! *(Throws a glass at Maria)* You slut ...!
(The kitchen door has opened and standing there, watching and unnoticed, are Dan and John)

Kevin: Stop Betty, she's pregnant ...

Betty: What was wrong with me? What was wrong with me?

Maria: *(Angrily throws a glass at Betty)* Non mi aggredire!

Kevin:	Maria! Stop it! *(Holds Maria)*
Betty:	Why her, Kevin ... ? Why not me ... ?
John:	*(Runs and holds Betty)* Betty, will you stop!
Betty:	*(Struggling to break free)* Bastards! Bastards!
John:	*(Hard to Betty)* Betty! Stop it! Stop this at once!
Betty:	*(Furious and clearly to John)* No, I will not stop – and you get your hands off me – what use are you? At least he did something – at least she's pregnant! At least he had the guts to do that! *(Breaks free)* Bastards! Every one of you! *(Runs past Dan, out the kitchen door)*
Dan:	*(To John)* Grab that one before she blabs this all over the place ...
John:	Right Da. *(Runs after Betty)* Betty ...! *(Dan closes the kitchen door. Stands. Kevin turns from calming Maria to nervously face him. A stand-off silence. Then)*
Kevin:	*(Nervously)* Da ...
Dan:	*(Furiously)* Shut-up!
Kevin:	Da, I ... (just want to say ...)
Dan:	Shut up! Shut-up and just answer me one question. Is she in the family way and are you responsible?
Kevin:	Da, can I just ...
Dan:	Is she and are you? Yes or No.
Kevin:	Da, is wasn't the way you think ...
Dan:	Yes or No.
Kevin:	Da, it wasn't a one night stand ...
Dan:	I don't care if it was a ten-day hopping match – Yes or No? *(John hurries in. Party sounds beyond)*
John:	It's okay, she's locked herself in the bathroom,

she often does that, but I told her not to say a word and now she's just crying and sobbing ...

Dan: *(Controlled)* Close the door, will you! *(John closes the kitchen door. To Kevin)* Are you the father – Yes or No? *(Moves)* Or do I have to go over to you ... ?

Kevin: *(Angrily and assertive)* No, you don't – because yes, I am the father and I'm proud to be the father – and it happened because we wanted it to happen, and I don't care what you say.

John: Jesus – I don't believe this! What's this going to do to me down at the school? I've just got my post of responsibility.

Dan: Shut-up John! *(Controlled)* Right, that's all very clear. Now all I want, on this day of all days, is to make sure that your mother hears not the slightest whisper about this ...

Kevin: Yes, exactly, if we just keep it among ourselves.

Dan: *(Controlled fury, to Kevin)* Because if she does, it won't be a clatter across the head you'll get, it'll be the toe of my boot into a place that'll make double-sure that this unfortunate baby won't be plagued by any brothers or sisters. Am I making myself clear?

Kevin: Yes, Da.

Dan: *(Louder)* Because you are a gobshite, a half-wit, a jackass, and after all we expected of you – you were the pride of this family ...

(The kitchen door opens and Doris stands there. Beyond, we can hear the party singing If You're Going to San Franciso. She looks stunned. Dan, seeing her, immediately continues)

Dan: '... He was known as Mad Carew by the subs at Khatmandu, he was ...' *(To Doris)* Ah come in, Doris – we're having a little anniversary party of our own in here. *(Fixing the table, clearing up)* Got a bit out of hand.

John: *(Helping)* Yes, and Kevin is translating Da's poem into Italian for Sister Maria – and doing a great job.

Doris: *(Closes the door. Controlled)* Good. Well when he has finished that, he can go up and pack his bags and he can translate himself out of this house as fast as his two legs can carry him ...

Dan: Doris ...

Doris: ... and he can take that young ... 'lady' ... and her offspring with him ...

Kevin: Now Ma, wait a minute ...

Doris: *(Furiously to Kevin)* Because I don't want you or her or any of your kind under the roof of this house for one minute more ...

Kevin: Ma, listen, please ...

Dan: No, Doris, you have it all wrong ...

Doris: No, Dan, I have it all right – because Mammy has been listening at the top of the dumb-waiter and she's been telling me everything ...

John: No, Ma ...

Dan: But Doris, you can't believe her – she's been out of her mind for years ...

Doris: And she is certainly out of her mind now – crying her eyes out up there, cursing the day she let us all stay in her lovely house, asking God for forgiveness for what has happened here today ...

Dan: Doris.

Kevin: Ma, please – I'm sorry – I really did try to be a priest, to do what you wanted, but when I met Maria, I suddenly knew that all I wanted was to be like everyone else ...

          (The dumb-waiter clatters)

Doris: *(Calls)* All right, Mammy, I'm coming up ...

Kevin: *(Angrily)* But you wanted me saying Mass and Benediction and giving the Last Sacraments – but I never wanted that – I never wanted to be different – I wanted to be like John and all of you – for God's sake, I just wanted to be normal!

          (Pause)

Doris: *(Ignoring Kevin)* John, please promise me one thing ...

John: Sure Ma.

Doris: That when you marry Betty, you will live here in this house, have your children here and, when we've lived out our lives and are gone, you will keep this lovely house in our family and not hand it over to be destroyed by strangers.

          (The door-bell rings loudly)

Kevin: Ma, for God's sake we don't want the house – you can have it.

          (The dumb-waiter rattles)

Doris: *(Calls)* All right, Mammy, I'm coming up. *(To John)* Do you promise me that, John? Can I tell Mammy that, can I?

John: Of course you can, Ma.

Doris: I knew I could trust you, John.

Dan: I'll go up with you, Doris, have a word with her – and don't you be worrying about this ...

John: I'll see if Betty is still locked in that bathroom.

Dan: *(Arm around Doris' shoulders).* This'll all work out for the best. You'll see. John won't let us down. We can trust John, never fear.

(Dan, Doris and John go through the kitchen door. We hear San Franciso *as they open the door. They now close it. The door-bell rings again)*

Maria: *(Tearfully)* Oh, Kevin, che cosa abbiamo fatto? E mo che ci succedera a noi?

(She goes, distressed, into the back garden and off. Kevin stands alone, watching her go. A moment. The door-bell rings again. Then lights change – and we are back to present day: Kevin's tie is done-up, he wears his glasses.

The kitchen door opens. It is Cecily. She is now dressed for the party)

Cecily: Dad! Did you not hear the door-bell – someone has arrived for the Golden Anniversary – some old friend of Grandma and Grandad.

Kevin: Oh, right. Thank you, Cecily. And is your mother still in the bathroom, having her soak?

Cecily: No, she's getting dressed, she'll be down in a minute – but Grandma said you're to answer the door ... and show them in here and get the party going. Quick. *(Goes)*

Kevin: In here? Right. *(Looks around)* Better do it so.

(The door-bell rings again. Calls) Coming.

(He goes to answer it, as we fade to darkness)

END OF ACT ONE

Act Two

Scene One

It is five pm. Same kitchen. But we now see it as it looks today – not as remembered twenty-five years ago in Act One.

The range is now electrical. The fuel-room is a laundry-room with a washing machine inside. The dumb-waiter remains, as before. However, the room-bells are gone. There is now a dish-washer and a microwave. The pictures have been replaced by more contemporary ones. A phone on the wall. Furniture is modern. The room is neater, more organised. Outside the back window, and close to it, a high wall runs the length of the house – eliminating much of the light seen in Act One.

This Act begins as Act One ended – with an overlap of dialogue in this new setting.

Kevin stands alone, his tie done-up, he wears his glasses. A moment. The door-bell rings. He pauses. The kitchen door opens. It is Cecily, dressed for the party.

Cecily: Dad! Did you not hear the door-bell – someone has arrived for the Golden Anniversary – some old friend of Grandma and Grandad.

Kevin: Oh, right. Thank you, Cecily. And is your mother still in the bathroom, having her soak?

Cecily: No, she's getting dressed, she'll be down in a minute – but Grandma said you're to answer the door ... and show them in here and get the party going. Quick. *(Goes)*

Kevin: In here? Right. *(Looks around)* Better do it so. *(The door-bell rings again. Calls)* Coming. *(He goes to answer it. A pause. Then Doris and Dan*

come hurriedly into the kitchen. They are as we saw
them at the beginning of the play – she is 71; he is
72, on a stick. He has a glass of stout)

Doris: Will you come on!

Dan: *(Coming in)* Doris, I'm supposed to be taking it
easy ...

Doris: *(Closing the door)* Did you see who it is? Pauline,
dressed up to the nines.

Dan: And what's wrong with bringing her into the
morning-room?

Doris: The morning-room! I know what I'd call it with
that disgusting picture looking down at us.

Dan: I think that's just a woman advertising bananas.

Doris: Advertising the kind of people who have destroyed this house. What would Pauline think,
looking at that?

Dan: Doris, Pauline is after burying two husbands –
she's a widow twice over.

Doris: And what does that make her – a sex maniac?
(Kevin comes in, calling back)

Kevin: Ah, here they are – this way, in here.
*(Pauline comes in. She is now 65, but glamorous,
and fashionably dressed – a woman who has clearly
not 'given up')*

Doris: Pauline!

Pauline: Doris! *(Kissing Doris)* How lovely to see you
and congratulations – I left a little something on
the hall-stand.

Doris: Thank you, Pauline – and just look at you –
you're like a film star.

Pauline: *(Merrily)* Ah but what film star – and now, Dan,
I don't want you saying 'Is it Lassie?'

71

Dan: I'm saying nothing of the kind, Pauline. *(Kisses)* Except I've never seen you looking better, whatever it is you're up to.

Pauline: Oh, that'd be telling you. But tell me, Dan, how are you, and your new knees?

Dan: Oh, grand, only they're now talking about giving me new hips as well. If this keeps up, they'll have me walking around like Pinocchio.

Pauline: Not at all, Dan.

Dan: And then there's the constant threat of blood clots.

Doris: Only if he sits around drinking that stuff. *(The stout)* But now, Pauline, what do you think of the old kitchen?

Pauline: *(Delighted)* Well now, Doris, I was just looking at it and I think it's absolutely ... (lovely).

Doris: I know – destroyed. I couldn't agree more. The range is a dud and they have a washing machine in the fuel room ...

Kevin: Ma!

Doris: ... and not a religious picture to be seen anywhere ...

Dan: ... and beyond that wall, where there was once the apple trees, they've built bungalows ...

Pauline: *(Upbeat)* I know, but I suppose times change and we have to change with them.
(The door-bell rings)

Kevin: Exactly what I say. *(Going)* Here's more arriving – though it could be Cecily's friends – I hear she invited a multitude of young ravers. *(Goes)*

Doris: *(Calls)* If they're mine, bring them in here, Kevin. *(To Pauline)* None of us are prudes, Pauline, but

	the disgusting picture they have hanging in that room in there ...
Pauline:	*(Merrily)* Oh, what is it of?
Dan:	I think it's an advertisement for ...
Doris:	Never mind what it's an advertisement for – I'm not having any of my friends coming over here to be looking at that and trying to drink tea and eat sandwiches at the same time.
Dan:	As long as they're not banana sandwiches. *(Doris gives Dan a look, as)*
Pauline:	And who else are you expecting, Doris?
Doris:	Well who indeed, Pauline – Rita McGuire is gone, Larry Heffernan is gone, May Slattery, and poor Myra Prendergast ...
Dan:	... who spent her life drinking orange-squash and her liver still gave out. It's a lesson for all of us. *(Drinks his stout)*
Pauline:	*(Then)* And everything is grand with you in Athlone, in the Residents Apartments?
Doris:	The Residential Apartments – couldn't be better, Pauline ...
Dan:	... twelve years this April ...
Doris:	... and we've now two caretakers and a doctor on call and they've extended the dining-room and our own little private house ...
Dan:	... with not a step to climb up anywhere ...
Pauline:	... and I remember the view from your front room ...
Doris:	Oh, the Shannon? It would take your breath away ...
Dan:	... just the width of it and when you see it first thing in the morning, with the sun shining across

it and the little cruisers sailing along ... give them a little wave ...

Pauline: ... and weren't you lucky to find it ...

Dan: Oh, a god-send, when we had to leave here ...

Doris: *(Corrects)* ... when we *left* here. *(Quickly)* But, Pauline, I can't get over how well you're look-ing. How do you stay so young?

Pauline: Between ourselves – I'm after doing it again.

Dan: You're married again?

Pauline: Married? Not at all – isn't my poor Cyril only dead four years ...

Doris: And we were always sorry we couldn't get up for the funeral ...

Pauline: Well, it was quiet, and very sad because he went as suddenly as poor Tim did ... but we have to live on ... *(Upbeat)* and, Doris, last year didn't I start going back to the tea-dances ...

Doris: *(Upbeat)* You always loved the tea-dances ... with poor Tim ... *and* with poor Cyril ...

Pauline: I did, and three months ago, didn't I meet Reggie Davidson at one. He's a northerner, lives in Lur-gan and recently divorced ...

Doris: *(Disapproving)* Divorced?

Pauline: *(Backtracking)* ... and I didn't like to hear that either – but it's only for companionship, be-cause nobody could ever take the place of poor Cyril ...

Doris: ... of course not ...

Pauline: ... and I know Lurgan is a bit of a distance – but the way we work it is: this fortnight Reggie comes down to me and the next fortnight I go up to Reggie.

74

Dan: Home and away, Pauline. Just like Manchester United.

Pauline: Always the joker, Dan. *(Hushed)* And tell me quickly now, are Kevin's children still living here or what?

Doris: No, no, only Cecily is here with herself. Paulo went to London and Stephen is at boarding school.

Pauline: *(Impressed)* Oh, excuse me.

Doris: Oh, the money pours in from Italy for their little pet.

Dan: Oh, not short of a few lire – but don't drink any of their wine. They send us over the odd bottle at Christmas – three months later your stomach is still reminding you.

Doris: Only because you never let yourself get used to it. *(To Pauline)* And, in case you haven't noticed, the poor child is now pregnant.

Pauline: Who – Maria?

Doris: Maria? How could Maria be – Kevin has nothing to do with her now. Cecily! And she's as happy as Larry and not a sign of the father.

Dan: And you daren't ask where he is. She'd ate you.

Pauline: *(Knowledgeably)* Oh, but that's all the go now – the young ones are now collecting babies like pets, and the young fellas only queuing up to oblige them.

(Kevin comes in, he carries beer to the fridge. In a good mood)

Kevin: No one at all for you, Ma – all youngsters, Cecily's friends, including two fellows with guitars – seems Cecily told them it'd be a sing-song.

Dan: Oh, grand. And no sign of the you-know-what?

Kevin: The what, Da?

Dan: The father of Cecily's ... you know.

Kevin: What? Oh no, no – I wouldn't say she's expecting him, as far as I know.

Doris: Indeed. *(To Kevin)* And is your wife coming down at all?

Kevin: *(Annoyed)* Ma, her name is Maria and she'll be down any minute now.

Pauline: Lovely. And Kevin, you have a nice place of your own now, have you?

Kevin: What? Oh yes, Mrs McBride, I have.

Doris: And left room for more Italians to move in here.

Pauline: Pardon?

Kevin: Some of Maria's relations used to come and go.

Doris: Or come and *not* go – with their singing and their shouting and their cooking and their taking over the place ... in case her ladyship was lonely over here.

Kevin: *(Then)* And Betty is well, is she, Mrs McBride?

Pauline: Pardon, Kevin?

Kevin: Betty – is she still in Canada or ... ?

Pauline: *(On her dignity)* Actually Betty is home, Kevin – been home, on vacation, for the past two weeks – in fact she said she might drop over to see Doris and Dan, before she goes back tomorrow.

Doris: Oh, it'd be lovely to see Betty again.

Pauline: Well hopefully. *(Then)* And I suppose John won't be home, will he?

          (Short awkward silence. Then)

Kevin: *(Unsure)* Actually I think he said he'd ...

Dan: *(Unsure)* I don't think ...

Doris: *(Finally)* He said he'd come over if he could.

Pauline: Lovely. And he's kept going, is he?

Doris: Oh yes – at present putting his pupils through their tests – he's very dedicated.

Pauline: And he likes living in Bristol, does he?

Doris: Oh, he loves it.

(The door opens and Maria comes in. She is 45, very well-dressed and attractive. Slightly highly strung. She has an accent, but generally speaks good English)

Maria: Doris! Dan! Oh, my darlings, welcome and congratulations.

Doris/Dan: Maria.

Maria: *(Kissing)* I have so many cards for you and presents for you ...

Doris: Thank you, Maria ...

Maria: We will give them to you at the special presentation later. *(Suddenly angry)* Kevin, why is everybody in here? This is the kitchen!

Kevin: I'm sorry, I tried to ...

Maria: *(Kindly)* And Dan, you are still very happy at the Shannon River?

Dan: Couldn't be happier.

Maria: It is so beautiful and the water is so good for the soul. *(To Pauline)* Oh, hello ...?

Doris: Maria, you remember my friend Pauline McBride, Pauline Boylan that was.

Maria: Of course, how lovely to see you – you will keep us all happy today?

Pauline: I'll do my best, Maria.

Maria: Like at the Silver Anniversary ...

Pauline: Oh yes – we thought you were a nun ...

77

Maria:	Yes, Kevin's idea, and so silly. And your Betty, she is well, she is happy in Canada?
Pauline:	No, actually, she is home, on vacation ...
Maria:	She must come over, we all insist – but you all love this kitchen so much, you all hide in here for what reason?
Doris:	Well it is lovely, Maria – all you did to it ...
Pauline:	Oh, it's magnificent ...
Dan:	And the lovely big wall.
Maria:	*(To Pauline)* Yes, so much land so my brother Enrico suggest we sell and build on it, get a good price and we all agreed with Enrico, yes?
Doris:	Of course we did ...
Dan:	*(Quieter)* Oh, there's no flies on Enrico.
Maria:	Maybe you meet Enrico, he is often here with my brother Stephano and his wife Lucia and their children – but why are you here, the party is in the morning-room *(Angrily)* Kevin!
Kevin:	They wanted to ...
Maria:	*(To all)* You come back for just one day and he does this to you? All go to the morning-room, all now, for the party.
	(The phone on the wall rings)
Kevin:	I'll get it ...
Maria:	*(To Kevin)* Leave it please! It will be Italy for me – and take everybody inside now. *(Into phone)* Pronto?
Kevin:	Okay, all into the morning-room.
Doris:	*(Close to Kevin)* And still led by the nose.
Maria:	*(Loudly into the phone)* A Caterina, come stai ...? *(Listens)*
Pauline:	Maybe it'll be nicer in the morning-room. *(Going)*

Dan:	*(Merrily)* You'll get to see the picture, Pauline.
Doris:	Dan, don't be drawing attention to it. And, Kevin, would it be too much to ask for some tea and a few ordinary sandwiches ... instead of what she has in there.
Kevin:	No, Ma, of course not – tea for ... three.
Maria:	*(Continuing into the phone, loudly)* ... Si, Cecily e qui con tutti i suoi amici e tutto cosi emozionante per l'anniversario ...
	(Dan, Doris and Pauline go. As they open the kitchen door we hear the crowd singing Oasis' So Sally Can Wait. Kevin puts on the electric kettle. Then gets bread, butter, ham to make sandwiches, as)
Maria:	*(Continuing on phone)* Ah Papa, come stai, stai bene? *(Listens)* ... Non preoccuparti per me io sto molto bene e qui siamo tutti cosi emozionati ... *(A loud laugh. Then)* Si anch'io ti voglio molto bene Ma ora devo proprio andare – Ci sentiamo presto. Ciao, ciao Papa. Ciao. Ciao. *(Puts phone down. Now angrily)* Kevin, what are you doing now?
Kevin:	They want tea and sandwiches ...
Maria:	Tea and sandwiches?! In there, I put all kinds of drinks, with Mozzarella crostini, marinated anchovies, squid salad, garlic bruschetta, ricotta cheese-cake, peperronata, pistachios – and they want tea and sandwiches! All right! Leave it, I will get it, if this is what they want! *(Angrily prepares it)*
Kevin:	*(Angrily)* Maria, I'm sorry if we have all disrupted your life barging in for this anniversary ...
Maria:	*(Busily and angrily)* Nobody is 'barging' – I am

delighted they are here.

Kevin: So delighted you couldn't come down to meet them?

Maria: I was having my bath.

Kevin: For two hours?

Maria: They were early, I was tired, I work for nine hours yesterday at the translation office.

Kevin: And no one else works? I had to drive all the way to Athlone and back while you were lazing in a ...

Maria: I am not fighting with you, Kevin. Your father and mother are welcome to this house anytime they like.

Kevin: And so they bloody-well should be – they still own it – you only have it until they decide to ...

Maria: *(Angrily)* All right! I know! I know what this is. I recognise this. This is 'Maria go back to Italy'.

Kevin: It is not. I'm merely stating a fact – they do own the house – legally they could just ...

Maria: *(Angrily)* So I will also state a fact – I would love to go back to Italy, I am sorry I ever left Italy, but I married you and I had responsibilities here, I have a family here, so I stay here – even if you choose to leave, Stephen choose to leave, Paulo choose to leave ...

Kevin: Funny how everyone 'chooses' to leave you ...

Maria: *(Emotional)* Everyone does not leave me – my father phones every day and he says 'Maria come home' – twenty-five years and he still calls Italy my home – they miss me, I miss them ...

Kevin: How could you bloody-well miss them – they're all over here!

Maria:	My Mama is not here, my Papa is not here ...
Kevin:	They were here and as soon as they left, the next lot appeared – it's a revolving door. But when my parents come, you lie in a bath...
Maria:	When *my* parents come, you move out to a flat.
Kevin:	Because they took over the damn place – and you may as well know that is why everyone else ran too – including my own father and my mother!
Maria:	*(Stops. Furiously)* Do not ever say that, Kevin, because that is a lie and you know it. We all know why your parents had to leave this house and this town, and it had nothing to do with me or my family. Do not ever forget that.
	(Kevin is silenced. Maria goes with the tray of sandwiches and tea. Kevin stands. He looks around. Then goes to the dumb-waiter. Opens the door. Looks up)
Kevin:	*(Calls up)* Hello?
	(During this, John has come quietly and speculatively in the back door. He is 49, looks older, hair grey, slightly dishevelled. He is now noticeably more introverted. He observes Kevin, as)
Kevin:	*(Calls up again)* Hello, Granny?
John:	Hello Kevin.
Kevin:	*(In fright. Jumps back, banging his head)* Oh Jesus!
John:	*(Amused)* Granny is gone a long time, Kevin.
Kevin:	*(Embarrassed)* I know, I was just ... seeing how it sounded. *(Then, goes to John, shakes his hand warmly)* John. How are you?
John:	Couldn't be better. And you? Still in the bookshop?
Kevin:	Oh yes. The religious section, would you believe?

John: I would. *Ad Deum qui laetificat juventutem meam.*

Kevin: *(Lightly)* Right.

John: *(Awkwardly)* I came around the back in case anyone ...

Kevin: No, no, it's okay. There's only Ma, Da and Pauline McBride inside. The rest are all kids, Cecily's friends, they wouldn't know anything.

John: *(Looking at the kitchen)* Jesus Christ.

Kevin: I know. All this happened after ...

John: I know I know ...

Kevin: No, I mean after Ma and Da left. Ma misses the room-bells ... and they never opened up Granny's old room, that Ma locked up when she died ... and the dumb-waiter still here, but doesn't work anymore.

John: Christ, that room must be in a right state up there – damp, wood-worm, God knows what. *(Disapproving)* And the wall.

Kevin: Da hates it too. The three bungalows are squashed in behind that. Remember the apple trees and the pear trees?

John: And does that really pay for Athlone – the rent down there and all that?

Kevin: Oh, easily. Maria's brother, Enrico, worked it all out.

John: *(Nostalgically)* Jesus, the old house has really taken a battering. Just as well Granny is dead – this'd kill her.

Kevin: *(Lightly)* Yeah – though sometimes, when it's quiet, you wonder if she *is* dead. Maybe still up there, listening.

John: *(Lightly)* And holding onto the rope.

Kevin: *(Lightly)* Yeah. She was gas.

John: *(Then)* And anyone ask about me, was I coming or anything?

Kevin: Only Pauline. Ma said you had students doing tests and you mightn't be able to get away.

John: *(Irony)* Students doing tests.

Kevin: She always says that. We all do. And nobody asks, they all assume ...

John: ... that it's a school – and not a run-down Driving Test Centre in the arse end of Bristol.

Kevin: *(Hopefully)* But you're okay there, John, aren't you?

John: Oh yes. Well settled in after seven years of taking my life in my hands with kamikaze learner drivers. But a ninety-per-cent pass rate ... and I'm anonymous.

Kevin: You were great to come back for the anniversary – Ma will really appreciate that. And Da too.

John: As long as nobody sees through my story – and starts to crucify them all over again.

Kevin: They won't. I'll stand by you one hundred per cent – one hundred-and-ten percent.

John: And they're okay, are they – Ma and Da?

Kevin: Well, Da's back on his feet with the new knees, but still complains. Mentions the words 'blood clot' every now and then.

John: *(Amused)* Oh, that's a good one! And Ma?

Kevin: Seems okay.

John: *(Then)* And is there ever any word of Betty?
(The door opens and Pauline comes in with the sugar bowl)

Pauline:	*(To off)* No, Dan – I'll get it. *(She stops, surprised at seeing John)*
Kevin:	Ah, Mrs McBride.
John:	Hello, Mrs McBride – great to see you, you're looking terrific.
Pauline:	*(Uneasy)* It's John, isn't it?
Kevin:	Of course it's John.
John:	Wouldn't you recognise me, Mrs McBride?
Pauline:	Well of course I would ... but you've got so ... (old) ... it's been how long now since you ... ?
John:	Ten years since I went to Bristol.
Pauline:	Since you went to Bristol, that's right. *(Awkwardly)* I only came in for some sugar, Kevin – your father says there's no taste at all from these crystally things.
Kevin:	*(Takes the bowl)* I'll have a look for the real stuff. *(Looks)*
Pauline:	*(Then, very awkward)* I suppose in all the hub-bub all those years ago, I never got to say how sorry I was for ... all that happened.
John:	Long time ago now, Mrs McBride.
Pauline:	Yes. And you're happy in Bristol, are you?
John:	Oh, it's great.
Kevin:	John's back teaching now, Mrs McBride – in one of the top comprehensive schools in the South-West of England. What's it called, John?
John:	What? Oh ... South-West Comprehensive.
Kevin:	That's the one. And are you the principal there or what, John?
John:	No, no – just a head-teacher. Head of the English Department.
Kevin:	Not bad, eh? – an Irish fellow head of the Eng-

	lish Department in England? That's real success. And white sugar for Da, Mrs McBride.
Pauline:	Pardon? *(Takes it)* Oh, thank you, Kevin. Good. *(To John, awkwardly)* And I'm so glad you're back into teaching, John. Betty always said that it was terrible, what happened, because you were so good with the ... with the students. So I'm delighted.
John:	Thank you, Mrs McBride. And ... and how is Betty, is she well?
Pauline:	She's inside.
John:	Pardon?
Pauline:	Betty – she just arrived. She's here on vacation, going back first thing tomorrow. Will I tell her you're out here or ...
John:	What? No, no. Maybe I'll see her later ...
	(The door opens. We can hear the party joyfully singing Past the Point of Rescue *as Dan comes in)*
Dan:	Pauline, the tea's gone cold waiting for the ...
Pauline:	Dan. *(Indicates John)* Look.
Dan:	*(Awkwardly)* John. When did you arrive?
John:	Hello Da. Just now. Came around the back.
Pauline:	And I was saying that Betty is inside ...
Dan:	Oh, she is, just arrived. Kevin we need one more cup and saucer – Annie O'Driscoll has also arrived ...
Kevin:	I'll bring them in ...
John:	No, no, maybe I will ...
Dan:	Yes, do, John – your mother will be delighted to see you – it'll be a great surprise.
John:	And who else is in there, Da?
Dan:	Only Cecily's friends, roaring and shouting ...

Pauline: *(Merrily)* And having the time of their lives – come on, John, we'll go in and see your mother and you can tell Betty all about your school – what's it called again?

Kevin: It's called South-West Comprehensive School, Bristol, Mrs McBride.

Pauline: *(To Dan)* Where he's now the head-teacher – and I'm delighted.

Dan: Grand. Pauline, I'll stay here for a while – I want to study a poem I'm going to say at the presentation. *(Takes out a sheet of paper – his poem)*

Kevin: Is it the one-eyed yellow idol to the north of Khatmandu?

Dan: *(Annoyed)* Why, what's wrong with that?

Kevin: No, nothing, it's a great one.

Dan: It is – but I'll have to learn it off.

Pauline: Well don't be long. And Dan, that picture on the wall – I see nothing wrong with that at all.

Dan: Sure I knew you wouldn't, Pauline.
(Pauline goes, with John, closing the door)
(Quieter) You must be well-used to that kind of thing by now. You and Reggie.

Kevin: *(Lightly)* Who is Reggie?

Dan: Her latest victim.

Kevin: *(Merrily)* Isn't she gas the way she ...

Dan: *(Angrily)* Never mind who's gas and who isn't – and what's this about John being the head-teacher at this South-West Comprehensive School in Bristol – where did that come from?

Kevin: *(Proudly)* Oh, that was my idea.

Dan: Oh yes, I thought it might be you!

Kevin: ... and luckily, when Pauline McBride asked ...

Dan: (*Angrily*) And do you think she's a gobshite the same as everybody else? You think after all she read in the papers when he got sacked and the court case and all the evidence printed in letters that high across every page – you think after all of that she's going to believe he got a job teaching in another school over in England?

Kevin: But Ma and you always said he ...

Dan: (*Furious*) We always say he has students, he's doing tests, we deliberately keep it vague, never naming names, so no one can ever come back on us. But a head-teacher in an English school! Do you want the whole thing dragged up again, and your mother crucified again and wanting to get back to Athlone and hide there where nobody knows her. Just when everything was going grand here, with no one mentioning it and she beginning to feel comfortable again.

Kevin: I'm sorry, Da, I ...

Dan: You were always the bloody same ...

Kevin: I was only trying to be helpful ...

Dan: Show you a heap of cow dung, tell you to go around it and the first thing you'll do is not only walk into it, but then drag everyone else in after you. As if your mother didn't have enough misery ahead of her. (*With difficulty*) I know I shouldn't be telling you this, but if you can keep something to yourself – which I doubt – you may as well know that she's ... not well at all.

Kevin: Who – Ma?

Dan: You may as well know that she's only been

	given, at the outside, four months.
Kevin:	Four months of what?
Dan:	Well hardly four months of a holiday in the Caribbean! Four months to live.
Kevin:	What?
Dan:	And that's only for yourself. It's not to go beyond you. John has enough on his plate.
Kevin:	But ... but who said this?
Dan:	The doctors, the consultants, the specialists, whatever you want to call them. She hasn't been good for years. It's always been on the way. Now it's here.
Kevin:	But I ... John ... everybody ... we always thought it was you who was ...
Dan:	If it wasn't for me, she'd be gone years ago.
Kevin:	What?
Dan:	It was me being sick, needing looking after – that's what's always kept her going. It still does. But even before I got the final news, I could see her going downhill.
Kevin:	And ... and does she know about the four months?
Dan:	She does not! And, by God, if you breathe a word to her ...
Kevin:	No, no, I won't ...
Dan:	Or to anyone! *(Calmer)* She knows she's not great: she gets tired – but she thinks she has a few years anyway. The specialist said if she knew she only had four months, she'd give in, the way her poor mother eventually gave in. *(Harder)* So Kevin, no making up stories, none of your cover-ups or your lies or your bright

	ideas, letting the cat out of the bag, on this day of all days.
Kevin:	Sure, Da.
Dan:	Just keep it to yourself – and let's make today a day she can remember for all the right reasons.
Kevin:	Of course, Da – but I honestly never knew she was ... she was ...
	(There is a sudden and ominous rattle of the dumb-waiter)
Dan:	What was that?
Kevin:	*(Fearfully)* It moved. The dumb-waiter moved.
Dan:	*(Fearfully)* What? Not at all. Sure who ...? it was the window rattling or something.
Kevin:	No, Da, it moved ... I saw it moving.
Dan:	*(Angrily)* But who'd be up there to move it – hasn't that room been locked up since ...
Kevin:	Since Granny died – even Maria never opened ...
Dan:	Then how could it have moved? And anyway that thing's been broken for donkey's years ...
	(The dumb-waiter suddenly jerks, then rumbles slowly up, out of view. As)
Kevin:	*(Stands)* Jesus Christ, it's going up.
Dan:	*(Afraid)* Stay where you are. Don't budge.
Kevin:	It was when you were talking about her ...
Dan:	About who?
Kevin:	About Granny!
Dan:	But she's dead these twenty years ...
Kevin:	*(Panic)* But she was always listening, she always knew what was happening ... and she's still haunting this bloody house ...
Dan:	Will you shut up! – she's dead and she's not lis-

	tening and there's no one haunting ... *(The rumbling stops)* It's stopped. It's at the top. Go over and look.
Kevin:	What?!
Dan:	Go over and look up and see if you can see up. *(Then)* Wait, it's coming back down again. *(The dumb-waiter begins to rumble back down. They watch as it comes into view and stops. There is a parcel in it)*
Kevin:	What's that?
Dan:	Go have a look at it.
Kevin:	Me?
Dan:	Before it goes up again.
Kevin:	*(Panic)* But why would it go up again?
Dan:	*(Panic)* Why did it go up in the first place? Why did it come down? Will you go over and see! *(The kitchen door opens. Maria comes busily in. She stops on seeing Dan and Kevin)*
Maria:	*(Angrily)* Oh, for God's sake – Kevin! Why are you still in here?
Kevin:	Maria, the dumb-waiter ...
Maria:	And Dan, why are you in the kitchen? The party is in there – I thought everybody was in there at the party ...
Dan:	Maria, the dumb-waiter ...
Maria:	*(Goes to it)* Why you open this dumb-waiter – now you spoil everything. This is to be a presentation to you *(Lifts the parcel from the dumb-waiter)* ... and now you have seen it. *(Closes the dumb-waiter door)*
Kevin:	Was it you who put that into the dumb-waiter?
Maria:	Such a stupid question – who else put it in?

90

Kevin: But that room is locked off ...

Dan: That yoke has been broken for years.

Maria: Yes, until my brother Enrico fix it.

Dan: *(Bitterly)* Enrico strikes again.

Maria: Dan, you say you have not seen this ...

Dan: *(Obediently)* I haven't seen it.

Maria: So stupid, Kevin – everybody inside being happy and you out here. Dan, you come in. The presentation in fifteen minutes.

Dan: Except that I have to practice my poem.

Maria: *(Loud and angry)* Practice in there and leave him in here, if he wants to spoil everything. Fifteen minutes for presentation. Come on!
(Maria goes, carrying the parcel. As she opens the door, we may hear Doris singing Bless this House. She closes the door)

Dan: *(Exasperated)* How in the name of God, did you ever get in with that one?

Kevin: Well, remember, when I was studying in Rome I went to Naples ...

Dan: For Jesus sake, do you think I need an answer to that question? Do you think I can ever forget those bloody, cursed days?

Kevin: Oh, right.

Dan: And even now, with her roaring and shouting and ordering people around, when she's not frightening the life out of everyone – and that voice of her's would strip paint off the wall.

Kevin: *(Then)* Da, about Ma ...

Dan: *(Angrily)* And will you stop going on about that – it takes me all my time not to be thinking about it, so don't start reminding me every five

91

	minutes.
Kevin:	But the doctors were quite sure ...?
Dan:	What do you want – a framed certificate signed by them all? Yes, they were sure ... and the second-opinion I got was sure too. Now, leave it at that! *(Learning)* 'He was known as Mad Carew by the subs at Khatmandu; He was hotter than they felt inclined to tell ...'

(The door opens. The sound of somebody singing ... as Doris comes in. She goes to get a drink of water, as)

Doris: *(Lightly)* Ah Dan, you missed me singing.

Dan: Was it *Bless this House?*

Doris: It was, in memory of Mammy and my throat is like sand from singing it. *(Drinks)* It was sprung on me out of the blue, so I just started off, hoping I'd remember all the words and I was going great until, half-way through, didn't my eye catch that disgusting picture looking down at me and didn't my mind go totally blank and I've no idea what I was singing after that.

Dan: As long as you weren't singing *Bless this Banana oh Lord We Pray!*

Doris: *(Laughs and drinks)* Stop! I don't know how I got back on track again. Pauline is next – she's getting very tipsy – and soon it'll be you.

Dan: And I'm going to make a right bags of it. *(Learning)* 'On the night before the dance Mad Carew seemed in a trance; And they chaffed him as they puffed at their cigars ...'

Doris: God, I'm nearly dizzy after all that singing. *(A handkerchief to her forehead)*

Dan:	*(Concerned)* You shouldn't be wearing yourself out.
Kevin:	No, Ma, you really shouldn't – you should take it easy.
Doris:	I'm grand. Come eight o'clock, I'll be only fit for bed, so I may as well keep going while I can. *(The door opens. Pauline comes in, in great form. She holds a glass of whiskey)*
Pauline:	*(Mock annoyance)* Well, thanks very much, Doris.
Doris:	What?
Pauline:	You walked out as soon as I started to sing.
Doris:	I was exhausted after getting through *Bless this House*.
Pauline:	Anyway, I got through mine too – thanks mainly to this stuff. *(The whiskey)*
Dan:	Was it *The Street Where You Live* Pauline?
Pauline:	Not at all – that's too old-fashioned. No, I did one that Reggie taught me – a modern one – *The Power of Love*.
Doris:	I don't think I know that one.
Pauline:	Course you do – *(Sings onto the high note)* ... 'Sometimes I'm frightened but I'm ready to learn, about the Power of Love' ... Reggie says every time I hit that note, it drives him wild.
Dan:	He's not the only one. *(Standing)* Look, if I don't get to learn this poem, I'm only going to make a complete bags of it. *(Goes towards the back door)*
Pauline:	No, Dan, I'm going back inside now ...
Dan:	Take your time, Pauline – this wall out here will offer little distraction. *(Dan goes into the back. Closes the door)*
Pauline:	And it's a great party, Doris – and aren't those

93

young people full of life. And Kevin, tell me, who does Maria be talking to on the phone, all in Italian?

Kevin: Probably her parents in Naples.

Pauline: She's on out there again now, talking to them with a parcel under her arm. Tell you what – I'll get her in to sing *Arriverderci Roma* for us – remember that – and save your phone bill. And you come back in, Doris, once you've cooled off. And isn't John looking great and his new school in England – as Reggie always says, everything always works out grand in the end. (*Sings merrily* The Power of Love)

(*Pauline goes. She closes the door. Kevin looks at Doris, who now sits, wearily*)

Doris: I don't know how she keeps going – the noise and the smoke in there would kill anyone.

Kevin: Are you not feeling well, Ma?

Doris: What? Course I am. I never felt better.

Kevin: (*Watches her. Then*) And you are enjoying it all – the party.

Doris: I am, Kevin, and more than I thought I would. To be perfectly honest, I wasn't looking forward to it at all, with one thing and another – but it's turning out grand now, with John here ... and yourself, of course.

Kevin: And do you often get tired, Ma – like, do you have to lie down a lot?

Doris: Kevin, I'm in my seventies – of course I have to lie down – do you think I pass my time doing jigs and reels? (*Her glass*) Here, fill that up for me again – save me from climbing to my feet.

94

Kevin:	*(Anxiously)* Sure, Ma. You just sit back there. *(At the tap)* And I wouldn't be doing too much in there – just relax and listen and we can go as early as you like, well before nine if you want. *(The door opens. It is Betty. She is 44, attractive, sophisticated, more contained than her younger self. She has a Canadian accent)*
Betty:	Mrs Gillespie ... ? *(Sees Kevin)* Oh, Kevin.
Doris:	*(Stands)* Ah Betty, come in, come in ...
Kevin:	*(Concerned)* Ma, you sit down ...
Betty:	No, Mrs Gillespie – they want you inside – you and Mr Gillespie.
Doris:	The presentation next, is it?
Betty:	Yes, that – and Mrs Williamson has just arrived.
Doris:	Ah Sarah Twinkle-toes, isn't she great. She wrote to me at Christmas to say she was having her left leg amputated ... *(Merrily)* she said that soon she wouldn't have a leg to stand on.
Betty:	Yes, she's in a wheelchair.
Doris:	Poor Twinkle-Toes – her dancing days are over now. *(Going)* She might need a bit of help.
Kevin:	*(Angrily)* Ma, for God's sake, you take it easy.
Doris:	Kevin, none of your shouting. And get your father in to see her – and tell him it's the presentation now and to have his poem ready. *(Doris goes, closing the door. An awkward moment)*
Betty:	Hello.
Kevin:	Hello. *(Then)* I only shouted because ... she really should rest more.
Betty:	I think she's really enjoying it all. She sang *Bless this House* for us.
Kevin:	I know.

Betty: She said it was the last song her mother sang up there. *(The dumb-waiter)* Do you remember?

Kevin: No – actually I was at the bookshop ...

Betty: No, do you remember her up there, shouting down the dumb-waiter, at the Silver Anniversary?

Kevin: Oh yes. Actually, this afternoon, I found the silver chimes you brought that day, they were over the door ever since ...

Betty: Oh, those? And what a search, to get silver for the big silver celebration. *(Then)* And next there was your own wedding.

Kevin: Yes. *(Shrugs)* A quiet affair.

Betty: So I heard.

Kevin: And how is Canada?

Betty: Oh, great. Vancouver is beautiful and work at the bank is really good, really challenging. So, no complaints at all.

Kevin: Great.

Betty: *(Looks)* And the garden is gone. The old apple trees. 'Whispering Hope'.

Kevin: Yes. *(Sings awkwardly)* 'Whispering Rope, oh Whispering Soap ...' *(Stops. Then)* And John is ... (in good form)

Betty: *(Quickly)* ... yes, he's looking great. Survived it all, it seems.

Kevin: Yes. You know he's still in Bristol ... *(Carefully)* now teaching his pupils ... in tests.

Betty: Yes, he told me – teaching little old ladies how to drive their Toyotas.

Kevin: Oh, said all that, did he?

Betty: Just to me, as a secret. I've noticed that people do that – tell me their secrets. Maybe they assume that, without husband or children, I have no intimate moments in which to pass on the information. Crazy, eh?

Kevin: Yes. *(Warmly)* Or maybe everyone thinks you're just nice to talk to.

Betty: *(Warmly)* Thank you, Kevin.
(Silence. Then Betty goes to the kitchen door and turns the key. She looks at Kevin, then goes to him, puts her arms around him and holds him. He responds)

Betty: *(Holding him)* This doesn't mean anything, Kevin – I just wanted to do it.

Kevin: No ... it's lovely ... I'm glad you did.

Betty: It's only for old times' sake, nothing more.

Kevin: I know.

Betty: *(Lightly)* So – do *you* have any secrets to tell me? ... anything since we got it all wrong in Kevin's Bed?

Kevin: Oh, that.

Betty: Or maybe that's just *my* embarrassing secret.

Kevin: Both of our's. No, I've none at all. *(Then)* Except ... *(Sadly)* Betty, my mother is dying.

Betty: What?

Kevin: No one knows. She has no more than four months to live.

Betty: Oh my God, Kevin – are you sure?

Kevin: Certain. She won't see Christmas.
(The back door opens and Dan comes in. He stops. Betty and Kevin move apart. Dan seems to remember something from the past, people even standing in the same positions as now – deja vu. He moves to the

97

	kitchen door, as)
Dan:	*(Awkwardly)* Beg your pardon ... just going into the other room ... going to say me poem ... and for the presentation.
Kevin:	*(Embarrassed)* Sure Da – sorry – this is Betty Boylan.
Dan:	I know it's Betty Boylan – hello again, Betty.
Betty:	Hello again, Mr Gillespie.
Kevin:	We were just talking ...
Dan:	Then don't let me disturb you ...

(Dan has reached the kitchen door. It is locked. He unlocks it. He now remembers)

Dan:	*(Lightly)* And no cigarettes or lipstick this time? *(Happily, to Betty)* Good.

(He goes, closing the door behind him)

Betty:	Does he know about your mother?
Kevin:	It was he who told me, in secret.
Betty:	God. *(Then)* I suppose, really, we should go in for the presentation ...
Kevin:	*(Not moving)* Yes. And you're well, Betty – like, you're happy and everything?

(The door opens. It is John. Beyond, we can hear everybody singing Auld Lang Syne. *The door is left open, so we continue to hear this, as)*

John:	*(Not surprised)* Ah there you are – Ma says you're to go in, Kevin – you too, Betty.
Betty:	Why are they singing that thing?
John:	It's the presentation.
Betty:	But that's for New Year's Eve.
John:	I don't think they knew *what* to sing. Maria is very emotional, Kevin, crying her eyes out.
Kevin:	*(Coldly)* Yes, she's good at that.

Betty: Kevin!

Kevin: *(Backing down)* No, I mean all her family are like that – emotional – they all cry at the slightest thing: birthdays, anniversaries, anything.

John: Anyway, you better go in. *(Comes in)*

Kevin: And you too, John?

John: No, I don't think so really.

Betty: John, you have to be there at the presentation – your mother is so delighted you ...

John: I know – but actually, I'm thinking of slipping away ...

Kevin: What? Away where?

(John closes the kitchen door)

John: Look, this was all a bad idea – me coming back – a stupid, ridiculous, senseless idea ...

Betty: No, John, they are delighted to see you ...

John: *(Angrily)* I know all that, Betty!

Kevin: No, it's true, John – you know you're the favourite ...

John: For Christ sake!

Kevin: No, you are – that's why when you ran off, Ma nearly went mad worrying ...

John: *(Distraught)* Jesus, are we now going back to all that?

Betty: No, John, but Kevin is right.

John: For God's sake, I didn't just run off, I phoned them ...

Kevin: Phoned them from the airport. You went from Mountjoy prison to Dublin airport ...

John: I had to have time to think!

Kevin: And two years before a letter arrived ...

John: All right all right, but I wrote to them after that

	and I phoned them in Athlone, I apologised for everything and I came here today.
Kevin:	Yes, but now you're going to run off again – and what's that going to do to Ma?
John:	*(Angrily)* Look, I don't have to answer to you ...
Kevin:	You can't – because you're going nowhere ...
John:	Doesn't matter – I'm going and that's that!
Kevin:	But there's no reason for you to go.
John:	*(Furious)* Okay, I'll give you a reason – there is a little bastard in there who knows stuff about me that even I had forgotten, who latched onto me as soon as I got in there with his bloody questions and his 'I hope you don't mind me asking you this, John' – calling me John, the bloody whipper-snapper.
Kevin:	But who is he?
John:	Says he's studying journalism ...
Betty:	For God's sake, he's probably only talking ...
John:	He knows me, he knows all about me, he must have read up every shaggin' newspaper file before he came here, hoping I'd turn up so he could ...
Kevin:	John, this is probably your imagination ...
John:	He's asking me questions!
Kevin:	Probably for conversation ...
John:	Conversation? Okay, what was his first question? 'I was wondering, John, when you told the gardaí that you were innocent, did you mean you didn't do anything, or did you mean you didn't know that the student was so young?'
Kevin:	Oh Jesus!
John:	And then he follows me out into the hall, waits

for me to come out of the jacks and when I told him to shag off and that I was set up by that same bloody student who wouldn't work and wouldn't study and who hated my guts, what does he come back with? 'Then how come you had those photographs – funny thing for a school principal to have in his filing cabinet'. There is nothing that the bastard doesn't know!

Kevin: Jesus Christ.

Betty: John, Kevin can go in and talk to him ...

Kevin: I probably know him, if he's one of Cecily's friends and I can just tell him to ...

John: Look please, forget it, leave it – I've made up my mind and I'm going – I can be in Rosslare for the midnight ferry, back in Bristol in the morning.

Kevin: No, John ...

John: Yes, Kevin! – and no more embarrassment for any of you, no more crucifixions ...

Kevin: No, John, wait ...

John: *(Going)* ... I'll pop over to see the folks, maybe at Christmas and I'll phone them as soon as I get back ...

Kevin: *(Anxiously)* John, you can't go off like this ...

John: I'm sorry Kevin, this has been one, major, shitty mistake ... *(Going)*

Kevin: *(Suddenly)* But Ma is dying.

John: *(Stops)* What did you say?

Kevin: She only has four months to live. Da told me in secret. Said not to say anything to anyone.

John: What are you talking about? Ma is fine, it's Da that's ...

Kevin: No, it's Ma. The doctors said it, the specialists –

101

John:	they all agree. Four months.

John:	Wait a minute – this is one of your makey-up stories to stop me from ...
Betty:	No, John – it's true.
John:	*(Then)* Does Ma know?
Kevin:	No. We're to keep it from her. *(Then)* If you leave it to Christmas, she ... she'd be gone. You ... you'd never see her again.
John:	*(Sits)* Oh Jesus Christ – poor Ma.

(There is a huge cheer from outside and the crowd singing For They are Jolly Good Fellows. *The kitchen door is opened. Maria runs in, crying with emotion – followed by Dan, Doris and Pauline. Cecily is last. All have glasses of wine. Dan carries the bottle)*

Maria:	*(Calling back)* No, no, no, this is private – only Dan and Doris in here.
Dan:	I haven't said my poem yet.
Maria:	All out – Doris and Dan now speak with my Mama and Papa.
Cecily:	*(Calls back)* Yes, all stay in the morning-room, this is private. Mrs McBride, this is private.
Pauline:	*(Merrily)* But look, Betty is here.
Cecily:	*(Turning Pauline)* Please, all back ...

(Cecily goes out, taking Pauline. The crowd outside retreats, still singing. Maria has gone to the phone and is dialling out. Kevin, John, Betty, Dan and Doris now in the kitchen, as)

Doris:	*(Calls back)* Pauline, you look after everybody – especially Sarah Williamson. *(Closes the door)*
Dan:	*(Anxiously)* Doris, I haven't said my poem yet.
Maria:	*(As she dials)* For God's sake, Kevin – why are

	you hiding in here with everybody?

Dan: Doris, I haven't said my poem yet.

Doris: Maria, Dan hasn't said his poem yet.

Maria: *(To Doris)* Okay, all right, he will say it now. *(Of the phone)* It is ringing. *(To Dan)* You will say your poem in a minute. Okay?

Dan: Out here? I should be saying it in there, where the crowd is.

Maria: *(Into phone)* Ciao Mamma – C'e Doris qui, e contentissima e si diverte e non e preoccupata perche non lo sa e tu non devi dirglielo – ti prego parlale di qualcosa di bello e poi Dan recitera la poesia per Papa ...

(As she speaks)

Doris: Ah Kevin, you missed the presentation ...

Kevin: We were talking in here ...

John: Ma, you should sit down ...

Doris: John, why weren't you inside? Why did you run off?

John: Sorry Ma, I'll go in with you now, soon as you're ready. Congratulations. *(Hugs her)*

Dan: *(To Kevin)* Did you see what they gave us for our anniversary – a crate of their bloody wine.

Doris: *(Quiet)* Dan, it's a special fifty-year-old wine.

Dan: ... and it tastes like fifty-year-old turpentine.

Maria: *(To all)* Doris, you here now, my Mama want to wish you happiness on your anniversary – you talk to her. *(Gives her the phone)*

Doris: In English, is it?

Maria: You don't know Italian – she speak a little English. *(To all)* Quiet everybody, Doris speak to my Mama.

Doris: *(Into the phone, in an accent)* Hello? *(Then)* Yes, me good too. How you? You good like me am good, yes? Me am thanking you for lovely wine.

Dan: Jaysas, Doris, now you're talking like Tarzan.

Maria: *(To Dan)* No, is lovely. Then my Papa wants to hear your poem.

Dan: What, into the phone?

Maria: Yes. And drink Papa's wine.

Dan: Oh, right. *(Drinks. Quietly)* Jaysas.

Doris: *(Into the phone)* Repeat again what you say please?

Maria: *(To Betty)* Why you all in here?

Betty: We'll be going inside now, Maria.

Doris: *(Into phone)* That very nice, but that not possible.

Maria: *(To Doris, suddenly angry)* No, no, it *is* possible, you say *is* possible, *is* possible.

Doris: *(Into phone)* Sorry – *is* possible, *is* possible.

Maria: Good.

Doris: And grazie to you too. *(Puzzled to Maria)* She said 'speek-a-dan speek-a-dan' – what does speek-a-dan mean?

Maria: Okay. *(Takes the phone. Into it)* Okay Papa, you now speak a Dan.

Doris: Oh, I see. Dan, you're on next – and they're all crying their eyes out over there.

Maria: *(To Doris)* Yes, crying because they love you and Dan on this anniversary. Now Dan, you speak to Papa your poem – he understands some English.

Dan: Right. *(Into phone)* Hello Papa? *(Then)* Right, here goes. *(With feeling)* 'There's a one-eyed yellow idol to the North of Khatmandu; There's a little

104

marble cross below the ...' *(Stops)* I beg your pardon? *(To Doris)* He wants to know whereabouts in Ireland is Khatmandu? What the blazes does it matter where it is?

Maria: I'll tell him. *(Takes the phone)* No, Papa, please, it is a poem. You no ask questions, you just listen. *(To Dan)* Okay, speak it now – Papa no talk, only listen.

(Dan will now recite the poem into the phone, as)

Doris: Maria, what was your mother talking about?

Maria: It is okay – do not worry, I explain – now everybody, we all go back inside to the party.

Doris: Grand – and, John, maybe you'll sing a song for us, or give us a poem.

John: Course I will, Ma.

Kevin: *(To John)* And then you show me the fellow ...

John: Doesn't matter – to hell with it.

Maria: Please please, all inside ... nobody in kitchen.

Doris: Shouldn't we wait for Dan ...?

(All turn to see that Dan has stopped reciting and is looking silently at the phone)

Maria: Dan, you finish your poem for Papa?

Dan: No – I was only half-way through when he burst out crying and put the phone down.

Maria: Good, that means he loved it. All inside.

Betty: Come on, John. *(Her arm around John. We hear party sounds as they go)*

Maria: Kevin, one moment please.

Dan: *(Going, to Doris)* Bawling his bloody eyes out – I could hardly hear myself talking.

Doris: *(To Dan)* It *is* a sad poem, Dan.

Dan: Jaysas, Doris, it's not *that* sad.

> *(They have all gone, except Maria and Kevin. Maria closes the door)*

Kevin: *(Annoyed)* Okay, so we weren't supposed to be in the kitchen ...

Maria: To hell with the kitchen ...

Kevin: Ah, you've something else to fight about?

Maria: This is not a fight – this is about your parents and my parents and they are all old people – now your parents' anniversary of fifty years and soon my parents' anniversary of fifty years ...

Kevin: Maria, are you drunk?

Maria: *(Emotional)* ... and my parents only want to live to see the little children of their children grow up but they know that soon they will die ...

Kevin: I see – you *are* drunk.

Maria: *(Angrily)* And Kevin, I do not like you and I do not love you and when we marry it was the greatest mistake because maybe you should be a priest or something else because you are a bad husband and a bad father, and a bad friend and a bad lover ...

Kevin: Okay – you talk to yourself here. *(Going)*

Maria: But I know your mother is dying.

Kevin: *(Stops)* Who told you that? Were you listening outside this door when ..?

Maria: Not the door – but like the old woman who died here, at the top of the dummy-waiter I heard your father telling you when I send the present down. So I know. Four months.

Kevin: Christ. Listen, you better not tell my mother ...

Maria: I am not so stupid. I only tell *my* mother and my father and they will tell nobody.

106

Kevin: So that's why they were bawling their eyes out.
Jesus, when Da finds out that you know and
they know ...!

Maria: He will be happy when I tell him – because
when I told my parents they cry so much and
they say that, for four months, your mother will
stay here, in this house, her house, maybe in
that room, with her own dummy-waiter – the
way she want it, not in that Athlone place that
she run away to.

Kevin: Maria, this is rubbish – they won't want to stay
here with all your family and ...

Maria: And for that time, I go to Mama and Papa in
Napoli and Cecily too and her baby is born in
Napoli ...

Kevin: Wait a minute, no way is my grandchild ...

Maria: ... and for four months nobody comes here from
Italy so your mother has peace here ...

Kevin: But who said she wants to ...

Maria: ... and only when she dies do we start talking
about us and our divorce ...

Kevin: Here we go again.

Maria: *(Harder)* ... because this has been a bad life for
me ...

Kevin: And what about me?

Maria: But your mother will never know of our divorce.
My Mama says let her die here, happy, not knowing. And all of this your father will like, for your
mother's sake, when I tell him. Now, stop this
stupid hiding in here and come in to the party
and sing songs with all of us and make them
happy, before it is all too late for everybody.

(Maria goes angrily. As she goes, she leaves the door open. We hear a rousing version of The Power of Love *– Pauline and everyone singing.*

Kevin stands listening. Then suddenly angry, he goes to the door and slams it. Immediately, the door of the dumb-waiter springs open. Perhaps it was the vibration of the slammed door – but Kevin is unsure, afraid, as he looks at the dumb-waiter ... as we go quickly to darkness.

END OF ACT TWO. SCENE ONE

ACT TWO

SCENE TWO

It is some hours later – almost 8.00 pm. Getting dark outside, so lights on. The party is over. Betty is alone in the kitchen, drying the last of the glasses and cutlery. Cecily comes in, she has her coat on.

Cecily: Betty, I'm away now.

Betty: *(Lightly)* Ah, the young ones off to greener pastures.

Cecily: No, no, it was a terrific party – but it's only gone eight, so we're going down to the pub – you're welcome to come along.

Betty: I don't think so.

Cecily: No, honestly – a few of the older crowd are coming – Mum said she might come later ...

Betty: Well actually, I think I'm my mother's taxi home ... and that could be soon.

Cecily: Yes, most of the old folk are gone already ...

Betty: Not Dan and Doris?

Cecily: No – mum is showing them around the house – it's great news: Mum says they'll have a fabulous holiday here, in their old house, for four whole months.

Betty: And you and your mother off to Italy?

Cecily: Yes, she's really looking forward to getting back to 'la famiglia Italiano'.

Betty: I suppose. Anyway, I won't keep you ... *(Shakes hands)*

Cecily: Nice to meet you – and safe back to Canada.

Betty: Thanks and good luck with the baby – in Naples.

Cecily: The poor thing will be cuddled to death. You know Italians! *(As she goes, Kevin comes in)* See you, Dad. *(Goes)*

Kevin: What? Oh, right, Cecily. *(To Betty)* Where's she off to?

Betty: The pub. *(Then)* She mentioned Naples – herself and Maria.

Kevin: *(Helping to put away glasses/cutlery)* Oh yes. My mother loved the holiday idea, jumped at the mention of it – more than I thought she would ... but the house to themselves, no Italians, nobody mentioning John or anything, that convinced her. *(Then)* If only she knew. Break your bloody heart.

Betty: It was very nice of Maria, and her parents. And Cecily doesn't know the real reason?

Kevin: No, and she won't until ... *(Stops. Then)* John said he'd drive them back tonight.

Betty: To Athlone?

Kevin: Yes – said he wants some time with them.

Betty: Oh, that's good.

Kevin: Then he's driving direct to Rosslare. He'll be back again to see Ma before ... *(Stops)*

Betty: Good.

(Both suddenly aware of the intimacy of this domestic situation – almost what might have been)

Kevin: Betty?

Betty: *(Aware)* And the answer, Kevin, is 'no'.

Kevin: *(Lightly)* I didn't ask any question.

Betty: I know you – and what happened earlier was exactly what I said it was – for old times' sake, nothing more.

Kevin: No, I know that – but all I'm saying is that it showed me that maybe we ...

Betty: *(Sternly)* No, Kevin, no and no again.

Kevin: *(Backing down)* Right, and you're right – I just mean ... *(Stops. Then)* But I'd always like to know that you're happy – like, there *is* someone in Canada, is there?

Betty: *(Lightly)* Ah, the question at last.

Kevin: No, I'm only ...

Betty: And the answer is, Kevin – I'm perfectly happy in Canada, happy with my life and happy in all my decisions *(Harder)* ... and all that despite the best efforts of you and your brother to turn my future into a prospective hell-on-earth. *(Lightly)* And is there someone? Did you seriously think there wouldn't be?

Kevin: No, no – matter of fact, I ... I ... I assumed ...
(The door opens. It is Pauline)

Pauline: Betty, I told Doris *(Sees)* ... oh sorry – will I come back?

Betty: *(A little annoyed)* No, Mammy – come in.

Pauline: No, I was just telling Doris I'd be off soon – but I can get the taxi I came in if you ...

Betty: No, Mammy, I'll drive you ...

Pauline: There's no need if you're *(Whispers)* ... if you're talking.

Betty: *(Sharper)* No, Ma, I'm done here – all finished and ready to go.
(John comes in)

John: Ah Betty, there you are ... *(Sees Pauline)* Ah Mrs McBride ...

Pauline: John. I was just saying I'm off now ...

John: Well no need to go yet – I can drive you home later ...

Betty: John, I'm driving Mammy ...

John: *(To Betty)* No, I can drop off your mother when I go with my parents ...

Pauline: I don't mind ...

Betty: Thank you, John, but it's all decided – I'm driving you, Mammy ...

John: But Betty, you could stay longer if your mother waits ...

Betty: *(Sternly)* And that's what I'm trying to say, John – I am not staying any longer, I'm going, with Mammy – we are done here and now we're going. Okay?

Pauline: *(Timidly)* I'll ... get my coat ... I'll be outside ... *(Going)* And good luck in your school, John.

John: Thank you, Mrs McBride.

Pauline: And I'll be seeing you, Kevin – and your parents – once they're on their holiday here. *(Pointed)* And I am delighted that they are coming back, if only for a holiday – because there was never really any need for them to go in the first place.

Kevin: Right. Thank you, Mrs McBride ... *(Politely)* and our regards to Reggie.

Pauline: *(Aloof)* His name, Kevin, is Mr Davidson. I'll be waiting outside, Betty. *(Goes)*

Betty: I'm sorry, John – I didn't mean to snap at you.

John: No, no – I just thought ...

Betty: Now, I've an early start in the morning.

John: You wouldn't stay for even a quick drink – for

old times ...?

Betty: No. Thank you. It's been nice seeing you again and good luck in Bristol ... *(Shakes hands)*

John: Oh, right, thanks.

Betty: And Kevin, I'll ring your mother from time to time from Canada ...

Kevin: Betty, there's really no need for you to dash off like this.

Betty: ... and good luck in all you do. *(Shakes hands)*

Kevin: Oh, right – and a good trip home ...

Betty: Thanks. *(Going, Betty turns and sees Kevin and John standing together. She suddenly remembers. Warmly)* 'Butch Cassidy and the Sundance Kid'. *(Betty goes. Then)*

Kevin: *(Quietly)* She's looking well.

John: Looking great. Think she'll stay in Canada?

Kevin: Unless Pauline gets sick or something.

John: Right. *(Now with difficulty)* Kev, I know we never really talked about this – but, what the little bastard was saying in there about me ...

Kevin: *(Doesn't want to hear)* I know I know ...

John: I was stitched up, totally, the kid was out to get me and all the support came from all those jealous bastards who'd seen me getting posts of responsibility while they were left ...

Kevin: I know all that, John, it's okay, I know.

John: Right.
(The door opens – Dan and Maria come in. Maria carries an opened bottle of wine)

Dan: Here's the pair of them – *(To Kevin and John)* Doris is seeing the last of them off ...

Maria: *(Annoyed)* Kevin, Betty is trying to lift Mrs Williamson's wheelchair down the steps ...

Kevin: Oh, right ... *(Going)*

John: It's okay, I'll help her.

Kevin: *(Wanting to go)* No, I can do it ...

John: No, no ...

Maria: One of you, please, before Betty hurts herself.

John: I have it, I have it. *(Goes)*

Dan: *(Calls)* And John, tell Doris not to be standing out in the night air.

John: *(Off)* Right, Da.

(Maria goes to the cupboard where the glasses, plates, etc., have been put by Kevin, as)

Maria: My God, who put these plates in here and these glasses ...? *(Angrily takes them out)*

Kevin: Sorry, I ...

Maria: How many years and you still don't know where to put anything.

Dan: Don't worry, Maria, we'll put them in the right place while we're here.

Maria: *(Kindly)* You do not worry – you will have enough to think about, poor darling. *(Kisses his forehead)* And here, some more of Papa's wine for you. *(Pours and leaves the bottle)*

Dan: Thank you, Maria. *(Bravely drinks it)*

Maria: *(Suddenly angry, at the drawer)* Oh for God's sake, who put the good silverware in here?

Kevin: What?

Maria: For years you see me put it in the sideboard in the morning-room, always, nowhere else. *(Continues angrily, loudly and passionately, to herself, as she goes with the cutlery)* Perche mai ho sposato questo imbecille. Perche non ho dato retta ai

114

miei genitori quando mi supplicavano di tornare a casa da loro? Non l'ho fatto e guarda ora cosa devo patire!

(Maria has gone, angrily slamming the door. Dan looks after her)

Dan: Ah, she's a lovely girl.

Kevin: What?

Dan: Maria. She's one of the best. All she's done for us. Do you know I could listen to that Italian accent all day!

Kevin: You said earlier that it would take the paint off the wall.

Dan: Not at all. It's a lovely musical accent. That's why operas is always sung in Italian. Her father talks that way too – when he's not crying. And he's very fond of her – he'll be delighted to get her back. Pity about their bloody wine. There's ten more bottles of this stuff to be got rid of. *(Begins to empty the bottle in the sink)*

Kevin: Da, she could walk in!

Dan: Not at all. *(Merrily)* And that was a great day, Kevin – turned out better than either of us expected. And the best is yet to come, back here in the old house, on our own, able to do whatever we want – and away, at long last, out of bloody Athlone. If we had to spend one more day looking out at that shaggin' Shannon, we'd've jumped into it. Oh yes, things are looking up at long last.

Kevin: *(Unsure)* Sure, Da, except for what we know is going to happen.

Dan: What's going to happen?

Kevin:	(*Concerned*) Da, I know it's difficult but we have to face it – what the doctors and the specialists all confirmed about Ma, that she has only four months to live.
Dan:	Oh that? Don't be worrying about that. That was only a cock and bull story I made up.
Kevin:	What?
Dan:	That was only something I made up so as nobody would start any play-acting, start another hullabaloo, making her miserable on her anniversary. We already had one anniversary ruined like that.
Kevin:	You mean it was all a lie? That now she's *not* going to die?
Dan:	Oh, I never said that. We're all going to die.
Kevin:	But is Ma going to die in four months?
Dan:	Well how do I know? She could be dead in *two* months, one month. I don't know these things. I'm not God, you know.
Kevin:	(*Angrily*) But did the doctors say she's going to die in four months or not?
Dan:	That's what I'm saying – that was a cock and bull story I made up to make sure she enjoyed herself – and I had to move quick once I heard you making up your stories about the South-East School in Bristol – I could see where we were heading there. But, be the hokey, it worked – isn't she having the time of her life, thanks to me.
	(*Dan sits back, smiling and contented*)
Kevin:	Jesus Christ.
Dan:	(*Merrily*) You're not the only one that can make

116

	up stories, you know – the only difference is I can do it properly. Like, my story managed to get Doris a four month holiday here ...
Kevin:	I don't believe this.
Dan:	... it got Maria a four month holiday in Italy, and Cecily will now be surrounded by a thousand baby-lovers in Naples ...
Kevin:	And what about you making everybody miserable, thinking Ma is about to die?
Dan:	But who's miserable? Nobody knows except you and me – and Maria and her parents off out in Italy. *(Stops. Looks at Kevin)* Oh, you gobshite, who did you tell after me telling you to tell nobody? *(Louder)* Who?
Kevin:	Well, John, because he ...
Dan:	You thick – I deliberately didn't tell him ...
Kevin:	And Betty ...
Dan:	Good God – and who else? All the guitar players in there and maybe the taxi drivers as well?
Kevin:	No! No one else – just Betty and John.
Dan:	*(Calmer)* Right, leave it to me, I'll sort it out – you do nothing! I'll tell John, privately, once he's driven us back to Athlone. News like that will cheer him up, after all he's been through.
Kevin:	And what about Betty – we can't let her go back to Canada thinking ...
Dan:	No, I'll give her a ring early tomorrow, at Pauline's, before she leaves.
Kevin:	*(Hopefully)* Or I could do that.
Dan:	No you will not do it. You leave that girl alone now.
Kevin:	*(Almost pleading)* No, Da, I'd just tell her ...

117

Dan:	You've already caused that girl enough trouble, even set her galloping off to Canada, so you leave her as she is, now that she's happy.
Kevin:	*(Annoyed)* Da, I never ever meant to make her, or anyone, unhappy. All I ever wanted to do is not to worry anyone.
Dan:	I'll phone her first thing tomorrow at Pauline's – and you leave it at that.
	(Doris comes in)
Doris:	All right Dan, I think we're on our way.
Dan:	Ready when you are, Doris.
Doris:	Maria showed me where everything is ...
Dan:	Oh, grand ...
Doris:	And it's a lovely house, once you get used to it.
Kevin:	Well, it had to be updated, Ma ...
Doris:	Course it had and isn't it grand – with the clean range and the washing machine in there and the telephone so handy and the lovely micro-wave – I think I'll enjoy coming here now ...
Kevin:	Great!
Doris:	... especially now that I'm not dying anymore.
	(Silence)
Dan:	*(Realises)* Were you ... were you up looking at Granny's old room just now?
Doris:	I was, Dan – because we might open that up for us to sleep up there ...
Dan:	So you heard Kevin and me ...
Doris:	I did – and, Dan Gillespie, it was a terrible thing to say to anyone, tempting God like that.
Dan:	*(Angrily)* Well the first thing I'm going to do when we get here is to block up that bloody dumb-waiter.